Taking the World In for Repairs

Also by Richard Selzer:

Taking the World In for Repairs

Richard Selzer

William Morrow and Company, Inc.   New York

Pieces of this book have appeared previously in *Literature & Medicine,
Medical Heritage, Massachusetts Medicine, Gentlemen's Quarterly, Vanity Fair,* and
Grand Street.

Library of Congress Cataloging-in-Publication Data

Selzer, Richard.
    Taking the world in for repairs.

    1. Selzer, Richard.   2. Surgeons—United States—
Biography.   I. Title.
RD27.35.S44A38   1986   617'.092'4 [B]   86-8488
ISBN 0-688-06489-2

Printed in the United States of America

BOOK DESIGN BY PATRICE FODERO

To Jon,
Larry,
and
Gretchen

Acknowledgments

I am pleased to acknowledge my debt to Yaddo, the Guggenheim Foundation and the Rockefeller Foundation for sheltering and supporting me during the writing of this book. I wish also to thank Charles Schuster for his ongoing advice and encouragement, and Harvey Ginsberg for his unfailing devotion to the editorial task.

Contents

Contents

Taking the World
In for Repairs

Diary of an Infidel:
Notes from a Monastery

Wanderers know it—beggars, runaways, exiles, fugitives, the homeless, all of the dispossessed—that if you knock at the door of a monastery seeking shelter you will be taken in. A bed will be provided, and food and the opportunity but not the obligation to pray. Those inside will know it too, the monks, and they will act accordingly. After all, the most unlikely visitor has the possibility of having Christ within him. So the monks are taught and so they believe.

It is evening. I am standing on the pier of San Marco in Venice. If I have been fleeing, it is from no physical hardship, but only from the dilemma of life. In my haste, I have made no hotel reservation. For some hours I have traipsed from one *pensione* to another. No luck.

"What is that place out there in the bay?" I ask a stranger. I point to a small island, every inch of which is occupied by a great church and attached buildings.

"That is the Abbey of San Giorgio Maggiore," he tells me. All at once I know that it is the place I have been seeking.

● ● ●

Let it be said at the outset that I am no frequenter of churches. The very buildings have become invisible to me. So that were I to pass a house of worship in the street I would be unlikely to see it. Long ago I accepted the notion that faith is something given to selected men and women, like perfect pitch. It cannot be sought after. No amount of yearning can produce it. Whatever adherence I had to the concept of a hereafter had vanished at puberty. Nor did its departure cause me discomfort. I felt, rather, dis-encumbered. Unlike heaven or hell, oblivion could be approached with equanimity. (As for sin, I have committed my share and failed to regret it enough.) Truth to tell, I love sin. And magic, and the possibility of a grand mess, the whole place caving in. Which posture has caused me to stumble from one humiliation to another with some frequency. Call it impulse then or impertinence or just perhaps *nostalgie de la croyance* that finds me aboard the vaporetto, leaving the orange fire of Venice and making for the island of San Giorgio in the bay. "Just a happen," Emily Dickinson would have said of the trip. Later, the monks will say that I have come in accordance with a will other than my own. But that is the way they talk. We shall see what happens.

The approach to San Giorgio is from the west. Physically San Giorgio seems a dead place, without periodicity. It has a solid heavy look, a sinker. Or anchor. Yet held afloat by something. All about the boat, the lagoon is flashing with gulls and gondolas. At last, with a thump and a scuffle we are at the wooden pier.

"San Giorgio!" calls the boatman. *"Permesso, permesso, signore, prego!"* and he pulls back the bar. I cross the great stone terrace and rap on the door. It is answered by a monk in a loose floor-length black habit that flows about his legs.

"I am a wayfarer seeking shelter," I say. "I would like to stay in your guest house, *il foresteria*," I tell him.

"I am Dom Pietro, the guestmaster," he says in English without the least surprise. He does not ask my name or whether I am expected. "I will show you to your room." He pivots momentously and leads the way into the abbey. He does not offer to carry one of my bags. Perhaps the idea does not occur to him. Perhaps it is his unworldliness. Perhaps he is rude. The staircase is narrow and winding. Ahead, he is all grace and figure, while, clumsy with baggage, I bump and scrape to keep up with him. At the door to what I see is to be my room, he pauses.

"Enter, Christ," he says.

"Well, not exactly," I say.

"Four hundred years ago the abbot himself would have come to bathe your feet."

"How long have you been here?" I ask.

"We have been here one thousand years."

The room is not a cell but good-sized with a high beamed ceiling. A large casement window opens out to reveal the Byzantine domes of San Marco directly across the water. The furniture is heavy, Renaissance. The floor, marble; there is no rug. I count three crucifixes, a woodblock print of Pope John XXIII and an etching entitled S. Franciscus de Paola in a State of Ecstasy. The Virgin Mary occupies a niche by the door.

"You have arrived very late in the day," says Pietro. "It is just now time for Vespers. Come." I deposit the suitcase and typewriter and follow him down a long corridor, descend a curved flight of stairs, cross a foyer, and step into what proves to be the side door of a great church. Inside it is black. Never, never has there been darkness like this.

It is the first darkness, undiluted from the beginning. I can see nothing. Ahead of me the monk's black habit has become part of the immense blackness of the church.

"Come," he whispers. "We shall be late." I take one blind cautious step and pause again. A hand slips into mine and exerts firm pressure. We walk for what seems a great distance, then stop. The hand is disengaged and with a sweep of pale palm I am invited to sit. In a moment he is gone. Slowly my eyes accommodate and I understand that I am entirely alone in a huge vaulted building. Far away, two small candles, like stars. And like stars, they shine but give no light. I sit for a long time in the absolute silence. Slowly the church forms itself about me. I establish the site of the nave, the great altar. High above, an angel hovers in full finial display.

All at once, there is a barely perceptible noise, a soft rumble as of thunder. The sound dies without discovery of its nature or source. It returns, seeming to come from all directions at once, like ventriloquy. One moment it is subterranean; the next, it gathers from on high. Is it the wind? Tricking among the roofs and towers? A construction of the water? A vagrant noise from the Piazza San Marco? At last it emerges from its mystery, grows into a tremulous hum and solidifies into chanting. The music has no tempo. There is no breathing audible in it. No one voice stands out; it is the fusion of all that produces the effect. Long-held notes which at last modulate again and again in the calm rhythm of the heart. Systole, diastole. Something, I think, that must be performed in tranquillity, a kind of respiratory yoga. I am suspended in the sound. And charged. My fatigue lifts and is replaced by a drowsiness. The headache which has plagued me for three days is a distant muted pulse at my temple.

The chanting dies away as gently as it began. Once again there is the unanimous voice of silence. In a moment

Dom Pietro is back. I have no idea how long the service has lasted. Time, it seems, as well as space is immeasurable here.

"It is time for the evening meal," the guestmaster says as we leave the church. "When you enter the refectory the monks will be standing, each behind his place. You will be seated at the head of the U-shaped table next to the abbot. Stand in front of the table and wait. Soon Padre Abate will arrive. He will come up to you at once and hold out his hand. You must take his hand in yours, bow, and kiss his ring. He will then conduct you to your seat. The meal is taken in silence."

"Kiss his ring?"

The abbot is bulky but he is not obese. Rather, his body is conscious and suave. It has the gracefulness of power. His smile is warm, papal. Behind those hooded eyes burns a superb intelligence. When he holds out his ring I bob to it. Against my lips it has the unyielding smoothness of a ram's horn. I sit next to the abbot on his right at what amounts to a high table. The others are seated at the two long tables of which we are the connecting link. Scanning the tables I see that all but one of the monks are big, fleshy men; that one is candle thin. The monk serving the meal places a large tureen of soup on the table from which the abbot serves first me, then himself. The tureen is borne away and placed in front of the monk nearest me. This man takes from it and passes it to his neighbor. Now the abbot tinkles a small silver bell. One tink. And a young monk seats himself at a lectern. He begins to read aloud, in Latin first, then Italian. His voice, though monotonous, is devoid of weariness or boredom. I do not get much of it. The lives of the saints, I think. Or the Rule of Saint Benedict.

A cruet of red wine is at each place along with a small

loaf of bread, fat in the middle and tapering at the end, thus repeating the bodily configuration of its devourer. The abbot takes my glass and, holding the cruet of wine high above it, pours so that the red stream appears to have a solid permanence. Not a drop is spilled or runs from the lip of the vessel. The meal, other than the soup of rice and noodles, consists of hard gray meat encased in a jelly. I think of toads and half expect one to poke its nose up for air. I can eat nothing but the bread, wine and apple. The eating of such food could never be thought sinful. I think of the thousand marvelous restaurants in Venice.

The monks, even the thin one, pile their plates high. Looking neither to the right nor to the left, they eat. As they do, their faces take on the lesser intelligence of dumb submissive beasts. At least three are out-and-out gorgers, slurping, mopping, belching. I spend the time worrying my food into insignificance on the plate. Another tink! and the silenced reader takes his place at the table. It is the time for talk.

"You are most welcome to our abbey and our table." The abbot's voice is smooth and practiced, furry. "But you have eaten nothing." A smile shows concern.

"Please pay it no mind. I am famous for it."

"It is the rule here that you must finish everything on your plate."

"Then permit me to serve myself."

"It is my pleasure to serve my guests."

"But you all eat so much. One is not accustomed."

"Saint Benedict has said that he who works shall eat."

"Then I must have some work to do here. You must give me a job. I am not comfortable when I am idle and all about me are fully engaged."

"There is no work for you here."

"Then I am to be an ornament? Please, I am a doctor;

I can give the monks each a physical examination. Or, if you prefer, I would be happy to help in the kitchen or laundry. The garden. Whatever."

"No," he smiles. "You are not to work here."

"But I have always worked. Upon my tombstone shall be carved 'He kept busy.' "

"No."

"Then why am I here?"

"The reason has not yet been revealed to me." The small white hands part briefly, then rejoin, and I understand that the subject is closed. Well, then. I shall develop my unrealized genius for elaborate repose. If I can do no work here, so much the better. Like the poet, I'll loaf and invite my soul.

"Tell me," says the abbot, "perhaps you can help me. Is there an English word—*tempiternal*? I read it the other day. How does it differ from *sempiternal*?"

"I think it was a misprint," I tell him. He laughs. Just that, and we are to be friends. He fingers the bell, and we rise. One of the monks with his cowl at full mast and his arms hidden in his surplice recites a prayer of thanks. The others listen very carefully. No one in the refectory but bows his head and folds his hands into a long pale flower bud. Spying, I see the thanker exchange the briefest, tiniest smile with one of the novices grouped at the farthest end of the table. A private joke. Why does this make me so happy? The departure from the refectory is made in silence and then there is a procession that is very far from the kind of academic slouch which I am used to at Yale commencements. They go *en file*. Moments later they are cowled silhouettes merging with the night.

At the door of the refectory I am retrieved by the guestmaster. So far as I can tell, none of the other monks has so much as glanced in my direction. Once again in my room, Dom Pietro becomes the perfect chamberlain.

"The bathroom is just outside your door. No one else is permitted to use it during your stay. The armoire is fifteenth-century Florentine. The bed, too. Only the desk is Venetian. All of the icons are of the same period save for the amethyst crucifix on the desk which is thirteenth century. The bed is firm and comfortable. The pope slept in it on his last visit."

"I am to sleep in the pope's bed?"

"It was before his election."

"Oh, well then."

Pietro lifts one eyebrow.

"By the way, Dom Pietro, what are the rules? I must tell you that I am incompletely housebroken and do not want to disgrace myself. Tell me what I must not do."

"The only rule here is that of Saint Benedict and that, of course, does not apply to you. But there are three things: Turn out the lights when you leave the room. If you smoke, collect the ashes and butts and give them to me to discard. Do not put them in the wastebasket."

"Where, then?" He points to an inkwell made of horn on the desk.

"That will do fine. Above all, close the window when you leave the room."

"That's all?"

"And oh, yes, one other. You must eat everything on your plate."

"It was hardly Belshazzar's feast."

"Nevertheless, you must. It is the rule here."

"*Per la penitenza,*" I murmur. Pietro is not amused.

The temperature is frigid in this place. I am shivering and my nose has begun to run. In the morning I shall have to chip myself out of bed with a little pickaxe. I fit the stopper in the huge claw-footed tub and turn on the faucets. From one, there is nothing at all; from the other, a pathetic twine of cold water. While waiting for the tub to fill I go to the windows and push them open. Venice snaps open like a fan. Directly across is the Piazza San Marco and the Palace of the Doges. Below, the ghostly night traffic of the lagoon. My room is on the second story at the front of the abbey adjacent to the facade of the church. I shall be able to pick out this window from the vaporetto. I lean on the ledge until a huge black shape erases Venice. Silent as a monk the freighter noses toward Yugoslavia beyond the sea. The wind of its passage blows the smell of cuttlefish into the room. The spell is broken and I go to my bath. After half an hour, the vast bathtub holds three inches of cold water. For my sins. I strip and tiptoe in. There I crouch, not daring to sit, and with the help of a soapy rag, rearrange the dirt on my body. No towel but a regulation-sized washcloth. I air dry. It seems that my suffering soul is forcing my body to keep it company. No sooner have I re-dressed then there is a knock at the door. Pietro. Am I to have constant attendance?

"Ah, I see that you have bathed."

"In a way. Might you have a bath towel?" He goes to inspect the bathroom.

"But you have washed the tub. I am to do that for you."

"The monk does not live who washes my tub. My rule." He disappears briefly and returns with an ancient frayed towel that I could conceal entirely in one of my ears.

"Also fifteenth century?" I ask.

"Will you be smoking tonight?"

"Yes. Do you mind?" I light up. "I don't suppose you . . ." Pietro smiles and reaches out to accept. I light it for him. He drags profoundly and exhales slowly. I see that he has not had a cigarette in recent memory.

"Will you have a brandy?"

"You have brought brandy here?"

"One does not set out to explore a savage country without bringing something to appease the natives," I tell him. And pour two large hookers. He sips with pleasure.

"Padre Abate and I are the only ones who speak English. The others are not permitted to speak with you unless necessary."

"Do you have many visitors such as I?"

"Guests are rare here. The occasional priest on his way to Rome, a visiting abbot come to concelebrate mass with Padre Abate, and of course, once, the pope."

We smoke three cigarettes each and drink another brandy.

"It is strange," I tell him, "the austerity amidst these gorgeous surroundings, all this vast treasure."

"Not austere enough," he says. "We are too fat." And he taps his belly with two fingers. "I myself should have preferred a thornier path. But it was not given me."

"Whatever for?"

"The conquest of self is the more complete in a severe convent."

I am extremely tired. Pietro does not notice and makes no effort to leave. All at once, I am set rattling by the sound of a loud bell. It is exactly like the bell used to mark the end of a period in Public School No. 5 in Troy, New York, and, five minutes later, the beginning of another. It is a harsh, prisonlike jangle, meant, I think, to startle rather than remind. In a country full of beautiful bells it is the cruelest noise that calls these monks to prayer. At the sound Pietro stands.

"Compline," he says. "Come and you will hear me sing."

"Another time," I say. "I am through for the day."

"I shall not be coming to meals regularly," I tell him, "other than breakfast."

He urges me to relent and come to the noonday meal.

"It is the best one," he says. "Very good pasta, fish."

"No, I cannot eat so much."

"It is you who are the monk, a Carthusian. On a single loaf of bread a week."

He laughs at his joke.

At last I am established in my room, the noise of the tiny far-off world on one side of the window, and on the other side, the limitless silence of the monastery.

Once I am alone the feeling comes over me that I have lived in this monastery room before, as though this were not my first coming but a return to a beloved room after a long absence, an awakening after a wintry hibernation. The bed, the table, the casement, the floor, even the crucifixes seem to have taken on the kind of familiarity that belongs to the objects of one's childhood, everything unchanged, as it was.

On the pillow of the bed someone has placed a hand-printed card of the day's activities:

ORARIO MONASTICO

ORE:	5:00	. . . .	sveglia
	5:30	. . . .	mattutino
	6:45	. . . .	laudi/messa conventuale (cantata, concelebrata)
	7:30	. . . .	colazione (fino alle 8:30)
	12:50	. . . .	sesta
	13:00	. . . .	pranzo
	14:00	. . . .	riposo
	15:30	. . . .	sveglia
	15:45	. . . .	nona
	19:35	. . . .	vespri (cantati)

```
20:00. . . . . . . .cena/ricreazione
21:00. . . . . . . .lettura/compieta
                   (cantata)
21:30. . . . . . . .riposo/silenzio
```

It seems no different from my own hectic hours in surgery where bits and pieces of day and night are pinched off, each full of its own obligation and necessity, though unannounced by bells.

Morning, after the very soundest sleep. The bed, though narrow, is deep. It molds itself to fit the body so that one is not so much in it as of it. All night long there were the lapping of waves and the dark shapes of freighters gliding past. I have begun writing an essay on surgery. My plan is to work on it a few hours each day. I have just taken a seat at the desk when Pietro arrives.

"Padre Abate wishes to give you a tour of the monastery."

I follow him to the foyer just inside the front door where the abbot and four other monks are waiting. With the abbot presiding, I am led from one spectacle to the next: the refectory with its great ornamental lavabi, the twelfth-century cloister of the cypresses, a monumental staircase, a long pristine white dormitory with, on either side, the black doors of the cells, each with its little wicket. For spying, I suppose.

The church, designed by Palladio, is in the form of a cross with a cupola above and an adjacent campanile affording, I am told, the best view of Venice. The facade, facing San Marco square, is of the finest Istrian marble.

From the outside, the dome of the basilica is one big tonsured scalp. Inside, it is wallpapered with scenes from the Bible: the Annunciation. There is the archangel impregnating Mary with words. Mary, herself, looking up from her book with that "who? me?" expression on her face. There, the Last Supper. The Israelites collecting manna. At the head of the nave is the choir where the monks worship. It is four steps higher than the presbytery where the great altar is situated and which, in turn, is three steps higher than the main portion of the church. The whole is a great prismatic box where light and stone interact to produce something greater by far than either one—a conspiracy.

There is no stained glass, for which I am grateful. I have always resented stained glass, its way of getting between me and the sky, always demanding attention. Whenever I see it I imagine the wickedest sins being committed behind it. The building is made entirely of stone and has the coldness of stone. What little there is of wood is in the furnishings, the ornately carved choir, the crucifixes. The altar is decorated with a large round copper ball placed over four figures of the Evangelists. It is this that serves as the tabernacle for the Holy Sacrament. All this is explained to me by Padre Abate. To me this church is a vaulting paradise where voices ascend, multiply and are gathered beneath the dome, where pillars and arches stretch away and away in every direction into far distant darkness. Here is a building that is never still, but alters its angles and curves to fit each new position of the body, pressing against one until it occupies the heart. I am struck by the great number of angels placed strategically upon every ledge and mantel, a whole host *tenentes silentium*. It is too beautiful, too perfect, the columns too straight and soaring. Humility alone dictates that one wall be defaced, one pillar be pulled askew by ropes.

Several hours later we pass through a pair of immense carved doors into a great hall or throne room. It is a huge square space about the periphery of which have been set three semicircles of thrones in tiers, twenty-four in each, as in an amphitheater. Below and in the center is an altar bearing twin candelabra. In one corner of the room, a small black pot-bellied stove with a chimney. On the wall in back of the altar, a large painting depicting Saint George having just impaled the dragon on his lance.

"Carpaccio," says Pietro.

"This is the Conclave Room," says the abbot. "In the history of the church only one pope was elected outside of Rome. It was here that the election took place. The year was 1700. The College of Cardinals gathered to this place. These are their thrones, preserved just as they were. The name of each priest is carved at the back. There," he points, "the little stove where the ballots were burned while across the lagoon all Venice watched for the puffs of smoke. We are very proud of this room." Dom Pietro touches the abbot's arm and they speak together in Italian. The abbot turns to me.

"Dom Pietro has reminded me that you are still tired from your journey. We shall rest here. Please," he motions, "be seated."

Gratefully, I climb the first step to the middle row of thrones, walk in one, two, three and sit in the fourth. All at once the four monks turn to each other and begin to jabber, using their hands wildly. I know at once that I have committed a gaffe. Something Pietro neglected to warn me against. I spring to my feet.

"What is it?" I ask. "I have done something wrong."

Padre Abate explains. "You have chosen to sit in the place of the man who was elected pope in this room. You must forgive our agitation."

My relief is as vast as their excitement.

"A coincidence," I say. The abbot shakes his head firmly.

"Providence," he says. And that's that.

O twice elected! I sleep in one pope's bed; I sit in the throne of another. From that moment I have free rein to go anywhere in the monastery. Only the dormitory of cells is forbidden me. About them I am immensely curious. To think that tucked within such grandeur there are those little pockets of modesty.

It is only with Pietro that I can speak freely, converse. His visits to my room, made in the role of guestmaster, are frequent and prolonged. While, in the beginning, the unpredictability and duration of his presence were annoying, I find myself less and less exasperated. I tell myself that it is because he speaks English but I suspect I have grown fond. Honesty forces me to admit that I look forward to that soft rapping at the door, the inch of opening through which looms that great mound of black.

What a great powerful woman of a man he is. A diva bursting with temperament. Well over six feet tall, and hefty, with skimpy blond hair combed straight forward to conceal frontal baldness. Much the tallest of the monks, he holds himself ramrod straight, which accentuates his height above them. His voice is baritone with just the hint of brogue. He is, after all, Irish from Dublin. The eyes are Anglo-Saxon blue; the nose fleshy with mobile nostrils. When he turns to speak, it is with his whole body rather than his head only, as though he were on a stage and playing to an audience. It is a flattering gesture in that it lends the impression that his entire attention is given to you alone. Turning, he lightly fingers the material of the habit which he does not so much wear as model. Whereas the others seem unaware of their costume, Pietro makes every use of it to express himself. By carriage and mien he is apart from the community. In file across the cloister the heads of the others are downcast and forward. Pietro's head is down too, yes, but with the chin turned slightly to the side as though he were listening. The others are merely monks. Dom Pietro is pure figure. He seems to have come to understand this abbey with his body the way an old sailor does his boat—the shadows made by the archway, the exact step in the marble staircase where his voice echoes most thrillingly from the domed ceiling. And in these places he lingers to submit, encouraging the building to express itself through his body. In his company, I feel all the more an old clothes-bag.

"Everything we do is in the interest of unity and uniformity," he says. "Our identical habits, the way we walk in line, heads bent, hands hidden in the surplice. Such an unchanging rhythm sets the stage for the appearance of God."

It is the chain reaction of monastic life. They have but to look at each other moving toward glory with submarine grace and their zeal is fired.

"But your walk is different," I tell him. "I would know you at once in a crowd."

He does not hide his pleasure at this.

Pietro has been appointed to look after my needs. Whatever I am to see and hear will be filtered through him. To see more I shall have to stand tiptoe and peer over that massive shoulder. Each time he leaves my room I turn the crucifix on my desk thirty degrees so that, sitting there, I am out of the line of fire. Each time he comes his first act is to turn it back until once again I am a bull's-eye.

"When are you going to stop being so childish?" he asks.

"Never," I tell him.

"Padre Abate has given me permission to take you for *un passeggio*, a walk outside. I'll be back for you at half past three. . . ."

"Good," I say. "Until then I can do my writing." Whereupon he sits down, lights one of my cigarettes and begins.

"You eat nothing," Pietro accuses me. "You are all wrist and rib like one of the desert fathers. It would be different if you were fasting out of penitence."

"I was the runt of the litter," I explain. "It makes you finicky."

"You do not like our food."

"That is putting it mildly."

"What is wrong with it? It is tasty and nourishing."

"No, it is all some ghastly mistake you are making in the kitchen."

He flashes me a look of mingled exasperation and affection.

"Show me," I persist, "where in the Rule of Saint Benedict it says that the food must be part of the penance."

He laughs with almost physical violence. At this moment he seems less a monk than I do. All at once he makes a quick pass at his temples, raises his eyes and becomes holy again.

Three-thirty and Pietro is at the door. We take the vaporetto to the next stop and walk the length of the Giudecca, making a number of side trips into the small secondary streets. I am struck by the cleanliness and tidiness of the neighborhood. And the silence. Although it is late afternoon there are few people in the streets. The glow of Venice lights up our hands and faces. I see his glance turn sidelong at a window full of food. We stop in a bakery and I buy two heavy moist sweet cakes. We stand there as he wolfs his down in a state of enormous happiness. I give him half of mine and he does away with that too, snuffing up the crumbs. The woman in the bakeshop smiles at the naked pleasure of the monk. He could eat ten more, he tells her. As a reward he takes me to the convent of the Franciscan Poor Clares of the Most Holy Trinity. Or a name something like it. It is a severely enclosed nunnery where some fifty women live in abject poverty and total isolation from the world. The windows of the cells are slanted so that the nuns cannot look down into the street, only up at the sky. The convent is presided over by a quite beautiful abbess of about forty. She, like the others, goes barefoot. From behind a wooden lattice she visits with us. Pietro jokes with her in a familiar manner. She has a full-cheeked heart-shaped face with a dimpled smile and clear gray eyes. She passes a bottle of wine and two glasses out to us on a turnstile. Pietro fills our glasses and I toast her. She takes no wine.

"How long have you been here?" I ask her.

"Twenty years."

"Only Lot's wife has had a longer sentence," I tell Pietro in English. He relates this to her in Italian whereupon she claps her hand to her mouth and laughs.

"What do you do all day?"

"We pray. At night too. We are busy all the time, and very happy." It is apparent that she has foretold my doubt. Pietro and the abbess engage in a long informal chat in Italian during which they both bubble over with what can only be construed as unalloyed pleasure. It is the shared experience of prayer that binds them together. Once again I am a goy among the Jews.

Here at the Abbey of San Giorgio each room and corridor is aware of every other room and corridor. Perfect in itself, yet in perfect resonance. It is forbidding. And the whole of the island enveloped in solitude, cut off. What could have possessed the early founders to plant their abbey here? Were they fishermen, sailors by nature that must never be parted from the water? This glowing house, these walls and columns and cloisters that divide up the way of life of the Benedictines—no road winds toward it from afar. It reigns over no fields, only sparkles like a chip of bright stone in the lagoon. And all this doting upon permanence, antiquity, which to gaze upon is just as disheartening as it is to peer into the future. Permanence gives a feeling of oppressiveness to a building. Here is a fifteenth-century table. There hangs an icon from the twelfth, and beneath this little glass bell you can see a few strands of Saint Lucy's hair. So instructs Pietro, dropping centuries the way others drop names.

And what a sobersided business it all is. This routine: Vigils, Primes, Tierces, Sexts, Nones, Vespers, Compline, and those meals which are only variants of the holy offices rendered in gastrointestinal terms. Then at dusk two dozen doors close; two dozen bolts are shot. And we are enclosed.

The objects and furniture of my own room, although doubtless arranged without a decorative intention, have achieved a certain harmony. I cannot imagine them in any other placement, as though the only way possible were with the bed against the inside wall and the armoire on the outside wall next to the window, the desk in the center of the room with the horn inkwell at the far right hand of the blotter, the amethyst crucifix at the far left; the wood-block print of John XXIII above the bed, with the Madonna guarding the door. Each object keeping its exact distance and relationship, each respecting the singularity of the other, yet at the same time complementing the others, offering planes, patterns, buttresses and corners against which each can measure its position in the world. It is the deadest room of my life.

In the inner courtyard there is a collection of flowerpots each holding a plant of some kind. Mostly roses and camellias, but I see lilies and geraniums as well. They are grouped about a white stone Virgin whose hand is raised in blessing. This garden is presided over by Dom Lorenzo, the oldest in the community. He is also the barber and the infirmarian. So far as I know, he is unable to speak a single word in any language, at least he has never done so in my presence. Nor even cleared his throat. Still he is filled with the deep breathing that I recognize as contentment. It is good to be near him. After the noon meal I go to the courtyard to watch him work. Now he examines a camellia, stroking the leaves one after the other, lifting the stems on his thick burry fingers. Now he palms a brick-colored pot. And like all lovers he hums an impromptu tune. I am envious of his work.

Part of the courtyard is fenced off as a cage for a large orange cat.

"What is his name?" I ask Lorenzo.

"He has no name." These are the first words I have heard him utter.

Now that is real poverty. To own nothing, not even a name. Dom Cat, then. And what a dispirited thing he is. The cats I have known watch every leaf on its way down, hear the least click of a mouse's teeth upon a grain of rice. But this orange monk watches and hears nothing. He has renounced the world. I see that he is very thin. Don't they feed him enough? I open the gate of the wire fence and step inside. The cat raises his head. In the depths of each slotted eye, a blazing yellow cross. I go for him; he arches, snarls and backs away. Again I try, this time from the rear. I long to hold even that ugly irritable creature in my lap, would risk every scratch and bite to feel for a few moments its hum upon my thighs, its rough tongue on my skin. Now I offer a hand. He reels, spits and rakes it with relish, offering three red stripes in return. The beginning, they say, is always painful. Never mind, I shall try again. I cannot let him live and die without knowing once the happiness of a human lap.

When I leave the cage, I see that Lorenzo has departed. Against the wall, a pitchfork! Here, where there is neither hay nor manure. Perhaps it is there for me to murder the cat. More likely it is used by the monks to drive out their lust. Just at that moment an errant pigeon lights within the wire enclosure and steps to within inches of the cat, to which intrusion the cat makes no sign of having noticed. Is it blind? The pain in my hand tells me it is not. One peck at the sanctified stone convinces the bird of its miscalculation. Off it heads for the riper pavement of San Marco. One marvels at the ways of bird and beast.

Among the flowering plants in the courtyard I notice a small graceful twine of ivy. Its leaves are glazed with dust, the clay pot that holds it is whitened by mildew and caked with dried mud. I glance about to see. No one. Only Dom Cat behind his wire fence. I pick up the pot of ivy and hurry back to my room. Who can blame a man for taking what he really needs? Kneeling at the tub, I wipe each leaf with a damp cloth, then scrub the pot. Now, where to put it? I place it on the small night table to join *The Rule of Saint Benedict,* but it doesn't do. I move it to the desk. No. The floor? At last it sits upon the narrow window ledge. But there too the ivy is all wrong. It looks awkward, straggly, as though having intruded upon this museum, it has paid with its gracefulness. This room which hates, yet retains, me has rejected the plant. I am oppressed by its presence; a balance has been upset. Pietro knocks and enters. He sees it at once.

"Ah, you have taken a plant."

"It needed a haircut and a bath."

"Dom Lorenzo is both barber and gardener here."

"It looks terrible where it is," I say. "I'll take it back to the courtyard."

"Yes," he says.

Pietro arrives to collect me for the noonday meal. Foolishly, I relent and go with him to the refectory. Boiled beef floating in fatty water. I cannot eat it and that's final. Also a limp variant of cold cabbage with a cheese sauce. Altogether awful but I am determined and down a bit of it goes. The implacable sweet wine and bread. A pear for dessert. This last I devour ostentatiously down to the gist, hoping to draw attention from my wastefulness. Still the monk who clears the table holds up my ruined meal with a look of mingled sorrow and reproach. I dare not look him in the eye.

Padre Abate and I are chatting during the brief period after the meal when discourse is allowed. All at once, he is distracted by two of the older monks, one on either side of the table, who are enjoying a rather noisy joke. There is loud laughter. It is Balm in Gilead. But the abbot is annoyed. He waits for me to finish speaking; I see that he is no longer listening. The moment I am silent, he turns toward the vociferous pair.

"Piano! Piano!" he commands. Instantly the men are silent, abashed, deflated. It is a ruthless slice. I suffer for their humiliation.

"Do you love each other?" I ask the abbot.

"Oh, yes. We do. They are brothers. I am their father. Of course I love them. But they must be ruled, like all children." He laughs genteelly. I see that he does love them, but not the way my father loved me nor the way I love my children. He loves them the way a shepherd loves his flock, or a mariner his crew, without passion and without recklessness but with an undercurrent of mistrust. The abbot sees my embarrassment for the monks.

"One must not love the excess of laughter," he explains.

"There can never be too much laughter," I say. "The world is so sad."

"Our world is not sad. It is only silent."

"Any silence would be pleased to be broken by the noise of such laughter."

The abbot reaches for his bell. Tink! And the time for talking is over.

Monochromatic, narrow, undeviating are the monks,

yet how they stir my imagination. I want to know everything about them. Had I brought my dissecting kit, I'd
have scraped them down to the hair follicles, just to see.
But then, I suspect the direct, frontal gaze is less inform-
ative than a peep through the shrubbery or from behind
the pedestal of the Mother of God.

To Venice for more brandy and cigarettes. Also bread
and cheese. Venice is seen best by the myopic and the
astigmatic, which is why I move my glasses to the top of
my head. The elongation of the eyeball enhaloes the city,
lends it a radiance, like the glory of Saint Benedict on his
way to paradise. In such a light the least act is bathed in
goldish colors. The café where I shop is full of men barking
at each other like walruses but with an implied courtesy.
Two women enter. One is wearing a bright yellow skirt.
One of the men calls out to her. He says something which
makes the other men laugh. A moment later the women
have joined them. I cannot take my eyes from it, the im-
plication of it. How they animate each other, all the while,
it seems to me, considering each other's needs.

One day into its night, and again a day with all the
hours jumbled. I watch the monks cruise from the refectory after the evening meal like widows on some melancholy errand, and I continue my patrol of the premises.
Prowling through corridors and staircases, I come upon a
pair of great doors most emphatically shut. I open one and
find myself in the Conclave Room, the scene of my earlier
triumph. It is windowless and therefore dark save for the
light given by four candles burning upon the altar. I sink
into one of the thrones in the first tier, close my eyes and
drift toward sleep. Something keeps me from it. It is whole
minutes before I know that I am not alone here. A monk
is kneeling on the stones directly before the altar. Why has

he come here? It is not the time of a holy office. It is the time for rest and recreation. I am curious but wish not to be indiscreet. I lean forward thinking myself to have been unobserved. We are not more than a dozen feet apart. And a world.

Although I cannot be sure, I think it is Vittorio, the novice master. "A very holy man," Pietro had said. In the candlelight the face of the monk is made of wire and glass and wax. He retains only the smallest suggestion of human nature. From his mouth comes a continuous whisper, now and then punctuated by a sigh. It is as though I am watching through a keyhole the upward flight of a soul. I can make no sense of the words. They are whispered conspiratorially, the syllables like pebbles worn smooth by rubbing. He seems in a painful state, a delirium. I am moved by a desire to relieve him of it, to jostle him out of his nightmare. But even were I to shake him, shout in his ear, he would not budge.

His passion rises. *Aves* come foaming from his agile mouth. Next to his lips my own lips are cripples. There is something epileptiform about it—the trembling, the shaking. Has he eaten some marvelous drug? Hashish? Mushrooms? When at last he raises his head, I know the difference between a face and a countenance.

There is no speck of egotism in his love, while the love I have known has been full of nothing else. This kind of love would vanish at the first attempt to analyze it. Its existence depends upon participation in the mystery. I watch him exploring all the limits of his longings and feel in myself for the first time the painful absence of God. For him these visions are privileged moments. He has learned how to summon them forth. My own dreams come of their own volition, without the fanfare of prayer. What is it that he sees each time, all in ochre, burnt sienna, carmine and flesh? Does he hear the shouts of Roman soldiers, the footsteps of women on the *via dolorosa*, the hammering of spikes. What must it be like to feel trailing at one's feet the whole of the gorgeous Christian epic—immaculate, murderous, risen? It is a triumph of the imagination. My own fails me at this point. I have no visions. Only, now and then, strange noises in my blood. There are tears on his cheeks! In each drop, a tiny candle flame reflected.

At last, he crosses himself one last time, rises, and still murmuring, comes to sit beside me. He is totally relaxed, unselfconscious. He smiles, his face still moist. His teeth are white as peeled almonds.

"But you were crying," I say. Vittorio raises his eyebrows as though I had just given him news.

"It was not grief," he says.

"What, then?"

"It was the hard labor of prayer."

Laboring, then, toward that moment when abbey will stop being abbey and become heaven.

Sunday. I go to mass. A German priest has come to concelebrate with Padre Abate. There is an air of importance about the event. The community scurries to prepare. The presbytery has been chained off and seats set up in the center of the nave so that the rite takes place at a great distance. The monks file in. It is so drafty that a wind stirs hair and lifts the hems of habits. A little chain tinkles against a silver box. As if on command, puffs of incense rise from behind the altar filling each rift and corner. Beginning in small fire, they bellow into patterns of ostentation. Each dense head of smoke punches into the diluter curtain made by its predecessor. Upon the ledges, the wings of angels ruffle. The mass is a self-absorbed omophagy, a meal partaken of only by its celebrants and their acolytes. The rest sit or kneel, watching and waiting for the moment to line up and receive the consecrated Host in their mouths. From the distance the face of the German priest is golden and waxed, a thing of closed contentment. His lips boil over with Hail Marys, incense ashake in his breath. The chant reverberates, becoming distant and hollow, as though great earthenware jars had collected and reissued it. To dwell on Christ a dozen times a day and never tire of Him! It is like gazing at the photograph of a beloved. One never wearies of the face that each time evokes the same powerful onrush of love. The monk seems to me like a child whose father has long ago died, before his eyes had had their fill of him, but whose image the child keeps forever in his heart and draws forth at will. I leave the church in the middle of the service, go to stand on the terrace in front. I must leave this place, and soon. Something is closing in on me. I feel myself to be quarry, something backed away, to be taken.

The high water that has covered the terrace for days has receded. Here and there in the declivities in the stone, puddles of water have been trapped. They seem mysterious openings onto something rather than reflective surfaces that might give the world back to itself. I am drawn to these windows in the stone. They are like apertures into the past and the future, broken-off pieces of sky. In one, a gull wheels, its breast whiter by far, its eyes more glittery than if seen in the air. He opens his beak and carries the whole sky in it. It is the first time I have seen my reflection in weeks. I look for signs of wickedness. If bloodshot eyes and crow's-feet are clues, then the evidence is stacked against me. Otherwise, it is just a face bearing here and there the mark of an old humiliation, a half-remembered pleasure.

Away, away from this trance of an island and all that has and has not happened.

It is shortly after Vespers. The monks have left for the evening meal. Nearby in the gathering darkness I hear the sound of scuffling, breaths drawn in haste. I approach and find Lorenzo, the old infirmarian, on his hands and knees feeling about the floor of the stall.

"What is it?" I ask him. "What are you looking for?"

"Miei occhiali sono perduti. Non posso vedere."

"Your eyeglasses? Which is your seat?" He points; I find them at the back of the choir stall in which he had been sitting. He puts them on, all the while thanking me for the gift of sight restored, and hurries away. We both enter the refectory late to find that the meal is already in progress. I take my seat next to the abbot and murmur an apology. Lorenzo walks to the center of the room, turns toward the abbot and kneels, on his face an expression of abject remorse. He is like a dog who has misbehaved and now is begging forgiveness. For several minutes the abbot continues to eat as though the man were not there. At last he gives a tiny nod which sends Lorenzo scurrying to his place. Still, clearly, it is a rebuff rather than a release. Dessert is a handful of unshelled peanuts. The abbot cracks cruelly.

"Lorenzo lost his glasses in the choir," I explain later when talking is permitted. "I stayed to help him find them."

"Punctuality at meals is part of the Rule of Saint Benedict," he says. They are not merciful to each other, I think. Mercy is a rough-edged shaggy thing. The Rule of Saint Benedict is too sealed and gleaming. Any lapse, however human or innocent, will be warily forgiven at best. What is sought here is not illumination, then, but submission. When it comes to God, I prefer a certain discretion, a courtesy rather than this all-out, overheated embrace. Besides, sin, as is well known, is the shortest cut to Heaven. I must spend more time away from here. Tomorrow I shall go to Venice.

Only three weeks in the monastery and already everything is both extraordinary and familiar. The effect is to make me a bit giddy. I feel like laughing. The smallest thing tickles me. My room has taken on a certain liveliness. Even the furniture seems capable of expressing itself; the crucifixes have achieved a state of movement. The green brocade bedspread threatens to overflow the bed and spill itself upon the floor. I am invigorated by it. I see that the life here is meant to facilitate visions. Here is a building that has been built and decorated by man to lure God. Perhaps that is all that one can do. Provide an altar with candles and incense, then kneel and wait.

Just below my window spreads the great terrace at the front of the church. It is made of fitted square flagstones of marble. Here, in the evening, singly or in twos and threes the monks come to stroll and gaze across the lagoon at Venice. Who knows what thoughts they have? Now and then their faces take on a wistfulness. A longing betrays itself.

Although talking is allowed on the terrace, more often than not, out of long custom, the monks are silent. What is there to say? Only, they walk, pausing to gaze across the water, eating the golden mist of Venice.

From this terrace, steps descend into the water so that the whole island seems to belong as much to the water as to the land. Sometimes, at the highest tides, when the *acqua alta* covers the stones, raised wooden platforms are placed between the abbey and the landing pier.

Directly behind and beneath my room is the cloister, punctuated at the center by two ancient cypresses, and at one end by a white stone lavabo. It is the stillest spot that ever was. A cloister, unlike a park or an orchard, is not the place to sit and have a long chat. First of all, there are no benches and one can hardly think of sprawling on ancient sacred grass. Nor, somehow, are the carved hedges and colonnades hospitable to the chasing to and fro of conversation unless, I suppose, it be muttered in Latin.

One walks in a cloister. Up and down and all around, slowly, steadily, letting the thoughts turn inward until the mind becomes the very cloister in which one walks. All this silence is just as well, for I am quite unfit for chat. I don't know what's happened to my mind. It's become like a crocodile half in the ooze and drowsing. Every now and then it yawns and snaps shut around a wisp of thought. Then hours of cold-blooded lethargy.

Though sparsely populated, the abbey is crowded with presences, full of its own story, self-involved, and presenting a profound indifference to the world across the lagoon. Except for the two cypresses in the cloister it is so treeless a place—just bare buildings exposed to the eye of Heaven. Oh, for a bit of dim leafage to sin behind. And someone considerate to do it with. The inhabitants of this place have amputated the past, torn themselves free of their childhood. What fills that place in the mind where memory rules? They are unstirred by the nostalgia and sentiment with which the rest of us alternately console and torment ourselves.

There is the time of work and the time of prayer; the time of rest and the time of eating. It is an immutable order which prevails, a childlike rhythm. They are children but without the child's lovely ignorance of loss and decay. If they yearn for the farmhouses and boulevards of long ago, one can detect no sign of it. Nor do they miss the faces that were once dear and utterly familiar—parents, brothers and sisters. For them there is only the long, long present lived out in the company of each other.

Every day the coast of Venice seems farther away, receding. It is a perception that now elates, now terrifies me. The abbey is more and more a labyrinth into which I have stumbled and from which I either shall or shall not emerge. What was at first a troubled silence has become a sheltering hush. Having no habit, I wear what amounts to a coat of many colors—red polo shirt, blue jeans, green sweater and horn-rimmed glasses. In my present state of dishevelment, I should be unrecognizable to the mother who bore me. Yet I am spared the sight for there are no mirrors. Except in the rare puddle, I have not seen my reflection, nor have I heard my name. I have asked Pietro and later the abbot to call me by name, but they do not. I am always addressed directly but never by name. Soon I shall have forgotten it and be forced, like each of the novices, to adopt a new one. It is as though I were disappearing, receding into insubstantiality. Now and then I light a cigarette and let the smoke curl slowly from my pursed lips, studying the jet for evidence that I still exist.

Again and again I read *The Rule of Saint Benedict*. It makes no mention of the likes of me in the abbey. Hospitality alone explains my presence, setting aside the possibility of my being Christ. Or perhaps my coming is an opportunity to test their faith against worldly contamination?

The trick to being celibate is to forget that you are a man. Easier said than done as Saint Jerome discovered in a desert. Saint Benedict too had his problems. On the back of each choir stall is carved a scene from the life of the saint. In one he is shown building a monastery; in another, he converts the heathen soldiers; still another has him being assumed to glory. My favorite shows the horny old saint fighting off a serious attack of lust by throwing himself into a clump of thorn bushes. Best not to talk. In a week or so I shall be sporting a full rack of antlers. All you have to do is drive out your nature with a pitchfork, make a desert of your heart and call it peace. Yet I am struck by the evidence of happiness on the faces of the novices. I cannot fathom it. It is a gladness that can come from no human source. I mention this to the abbot.

"It is the gladness of heaven," he says.

Along with human love, what is missing here is reproduction. Nothing, no one is born here. There are no new eyes, new breaths. There are no natives; everyone has come from somewhere else. All the fecundity is in the long ago. It stopped at the womb of Mary. Sixteen men, then, full of unspent sperm, dry as chalk. By what magic do their faces remain unscored, their hair full and black, their hands youthful and soft? With what is their flesh nourished that each one looks twenty years younger than he is? As though he were being returned to the condition of Adam before the Fall. While, I, pouched and sacculate, am at the height of my beshrivelment. It is the refrigerated condition of their lives, I think, that holds back decay. Thousand-year-old insects trapped in amber share the same incorruptibility. I watch their shadows fall across each other in the cloister, one monk darkening another who in turn darkens the next. It is their only manner of touching. As for myself, I shall, in the matter of chastity, proceed day by day, secure in the folk wisdom that one does not go blind in the absence of sex. But, oh, to gather and spread a woman's hair upon my bare shoulders. Personally, I think it felicitous of man to have sinned his way out of the Garden of Eden which must have been claustral and dull. O give me Babylon or Nineveh. I am just a few days short of adding Venice to the list.

At San Giorgio instead of irony there is humility; instead of satire, sermon. Irony is the human glance. I am used to it. Eternity is the cool perspective of God. And this God is not ironic; he is earnest and high. This evening I return to the church, trying to feel what it is that is expressed there seven times a day and what lingers in the intervals. Faced by the passionate striving of the last rays of the sun and lingering wisps of scent, I have to remind myself of the inanimacy of stone. At such moments, I would

43

greatly appreciate a reassuring sign from heaven. Which-ever way I look I see carved an endless variety of sunlit patches—spaces, angles, arcs. In contrast to the dark half shadows below, the upper galleries deliver an atrium of light that transforms that well of shadows into a luminous cave. I spy on the monks as they chant, drawing as close to the choir as I can without disturbing them. Here, even the faces of the old have the tenderness of youth. They seem to listen as they sing, abandoning themselves, while translating the universe.

Back in my room it is quiet, quiet, only the quick small slide of my hand across the paper as I write. But my atheist pen is marching out of step here. I glance up to capture a thought, and through the forest of crucifixes see the bottle of brandy on the nightstand. The pen discarded, I stand at the window, sipping. Two gulls wheel; I call out to them, just to hear the sound of my voice. First one, then the other answers me. Well, good, then. I shall converse with the birds. Like Saint Francis.

I have been given the run of the monastery. Only the cells of the monks continue to be forbidden me. The complex of buildings is vast and the monks, engaged in their prayers and duties, are largely invisible. A whole day will go by without my meeting one of them. On the occasion that I do, the monumental silhouette floats near, lowers its head and hurries past with, at most, a whispered "*Buon giorno.*" More is not permitted. For one who believes that a good chat is the highest development of civilization, this interdiction of conversation is hard to bear. I miss that low hum, more audible to the heart than to the ear, by which a lived-in house announces itself. Sometimes, while sitting in the park or while writing at my desk, I have the feeling that I am not alone, that others are present. I know they are not. Still, I turn around to see. And sometimes I think—Good Lord!—perhaps the whole of the community

44

who lived here has fled, and to the millennium of spiritual influence, now I alone stand heir.

A great drowsiness has come over me, as though the air here were webbed and I trapped within it. I relieve myself of a dozen yawns an hour. As many as a monk does prayers. No sooner is one yawn expelled with jaw-dislocating emphasis than the next bubble gathers in my head. By tomorrow I shall be in deep coma. In such a convalescent state, for that is what I have diagnosed it to be, I can explore only by small ambitions, hithering and thithering as far as the Conclave Room for a long solitary sit-down, lethargic as a turtle on a sunny rock; on to the sacristy— another daydream; then up to the top of the companile where I feel like a muezzin on a mosque. Once again Padre Abate has refused to let me work. Oh, well, if there is nothing whatever to do here, then I am just the man to do it. Every evening I return from a ramble in the cloister to find that my room has been swept clean, the cigarette ashes taken away, and the bed which I had made, remade according to some fierce precision of which I am ignorant. Who did it? The angels?

Time and again the great church of San Giorgio Maggiore coaxes me inside her. I have taken to sitting there at odd hours. Truth to tell, I am far more attracted to the bells, incense and statues of a religion than I am to its dogma or Talmud. It is the child in me craving diversion. And this church is brimful of spectacle, what with John the Baptist shaggy on the wall, Lazarus half in and half out of his shroud, and, of course, Saint George in full metallic fig. In the absense of human beings I have been keeping company with the statuary. Just today in the church at twilight a gray angel soared over my head. I could feel the breeze of its passing. But what is this! In the midst of perfection I have discovered that one of the host of angels, the third to the left of the main altar, has been imperfectly rendered, one wing being rather too centrally rooted at the back, and more than a little lower in its thoracic attachment than the other wing. The corresponding shoulder droops, giving a kyphoscoliosis of the spine. Such an angel would hover askew, list to the affected side. Here, I think, is a cockeyed creature made from a bumpy hunk of marble by hands less skilled than willing. Still, something about her miscreation is endearing, as though her sculptor had not yet learned the dishonesties of art. I say "her" because of all the race of angels on this island, only this one suggests specificity of gender. Aside from Michael, Gabriel and the one who wrestled with Jacob, about whose masculinity there has never been any doubt, the others are sexually indeterminate. The gender of angels is not readily told. One does not turn them upside down to see. Nor is it of the least importance, as the whole idea, I gather, is that they be neuter. But this crookback to the left of the altar is, beyond peradventure of doubt, womanly—the female of the species. It is something about the elbows, the knees, whatever. Nor does she have the basic seraph's countenance with plump cheeks and serene brow all framed by ringlets. Instead, she is stringy. All wrists and ribs. The face too owns a certain gauntness of features, the suggestion of fatigue. The mouth is a thin slit; the expression is less one of ecstasy than of endurance. This face has witnessed; it has tolerated. Now and then I have the fleeting thought that I have seen this face before. But where? Whose is it?

It is three midnights later. I awake suddenly and lie there in bed rummaging about in what I used to call my mind. All at once, I am bolt upright. In a moment I have pulled on my clothes, grabbed candlestick and matches and am racing along the hallway, down a flight of stairs. I push open the side door of the church. It is full, still, of the sweet smell of incense. And, oh, that black that does not hold itself back but comes charging at you like a panther. I light the match, touch it to the taper. But why do my hands tremble so? I watch my shadow become involved with the dormant church as the flame is batted in the draft. The great altar looms; now to the left. One. Two. Three. And I hold up the candle at arm's length. Flashes of gold from the monstrance. The stillness rages in the very pillars. And I know. I am certain.

Some months before I left New Haven, a nurse who had worked in the recovery room retired. For thirty-five years, each day, Adele Cleary had received into her care dozens of postoperative patients, each of whom shared the single condition of unconsciousness, being either fully anesthetized or in emergence from that state. Upon leaving they would be amnesic for their time spent in this room. While one would flail about in danger of injuring himself, another, driven by some drug-released urge toward violence, would strike out at those who tended him. I remember one of her black eyes. Part of the job, Adele had said afterward. Still another patient would vomit or choke or suffer cardiac arrest and so must be resuscitated by mouth-to-mouth breathing, and receive a beating upon the chest to coax back a heart in standstill. Nor did a single one of her patients remember Adele. Were she, later, to pass one of them in the street, he would give no sign of recognition. To all of this Adele presented an unruffled expression. It was more than tolerance or endurance; it was acceptance, it was obedience. Adele Cleary was a hunchback. Despite the fact of her crooked spine, which was ill-concealed and even accentuated by the thin blue scrub dress she wore at work, there was no awkwardness in her ministrations. In the recovery room, if nowhere else, she was graceful. At her retirement she was presented with a purse containing one hundred dollars collected from the others. The chief of surgery proposed a toast with ginger ale.

"What are you going to do now, Adele?" he asked. "Are you going to travel? Or just loaf?"

"Now?" said Adele with a shy smile. "Now I am going to recover from my life."

I saw her once after that. There is a small park in the center of New Haven. It is called The Green. In good weather people go there to eat lunch, play chess or walk their dogs. One day I was crossing The Green on some errand or other when I caught sight of her sitting alone on one of the benches that line the paths. Several people walked by. All at once she rose and walked quickly to catch up with a man who had just passed. When she had come within arm's length she raised one hand to touch his sleeve. I saw the man turn, look at her for a moment without expression, then wheel and walk briskly away. After a moment, Adele returned to her seat. I stopped to talk.

"Who was that?" I asked her. We were that easy with each other.

"Oh," she said. "Someone I thought I knew. But I guess not."

"One of your patients?" I said. Adele smiled and looked at something farther and farther away from her body.

Later that day, sitting in my office at the hospital, I thought of her again, of how many thousands of people in the city she had steadied and thumped and rubbed and blown into; of all the vomitus and phlegm and blood with which she had been spattered; of all the prophecies she had sown: "You are going to be all right," "Pretty soon you'll be back in your own bed"; all her crooning, her coaxing back, her padding against mindless battering; all those magic acts of intercession; that endless braiding of tubes and wires about pale sick faces. And no one could remember having seen her!

Before I left for Italy I saw her name in the obituary

48

column. Isn't that just the way? You work all your life, and the minute you stop and begin to enjoy . . .

For a long while I gaze up at the statue of the angel, the third from the left of the main altar, the hot wax from the taper begloving my hand in tightness and heat which races up the arm and across the chest where the heart beats hard against it. Look! She bends to peer at me, lifts one hand as if to wipe a brow, then slowly relents into marble. So! Adele, I say aloud. I might have known.

Minutes later, back in my room, I snuff the taper. There is the sad smell of candlewick. And the singing of wings.

To search for faith in a monastery is to deny its existence elsewhere. True morality is directed outward toward others. It has nothing to do with self-perfection. Besides it is less what goes into man than what comes out of him that matters.

Take Dom Pietro. Eighteen years in a monastery and he has remained a personage. I can see him carried across the Piazza San Marco on a *sedia gestatoria* shedding benedictions on the crowd. Listen:

It is only months ago. I am visiting another surgeon's operating room. The woman on the table had lost the circulation in her right arm. Weeks before, a new artery had been grafted between her aorta and the blocked blood vessel. For a while, the pulse had returned to her wrist, but then came fever. The pain in her hand returned and the pulse vanished. An infection had developed in the graft and now not only her arm but her life was at stake. Wayne Flye is a young surgeon newly arrived at our hospital from Texas. This was to be his first operation in New Haven. I am present out of a spirit of comradeship. I want to keep him company. I observe now as he reopens the old incision

49

in her chest, splitting her breastbone in two. He raises the sternum as you would raise the two halves of a hatchway. But as he does there is a great bang of blood. In a moment the chest is full of it, with more lapping at the gunwales. Adhesions from the previous surgery and from the infection have been torn. But you could not tell from watching this surgeon. His voice is Texas slow, quiet; he murmurs to his assistants, the nurse. His manner is controlled, oaken, as though the hemorrhage had somehow strengthened his resolve. His fingers enter the chest, submerge. It is a gentle burrowing as they sniff out the site of the bleeding.

"Here," he says, at last. He has found what he was looking for. "Suction." And the lake of blood is drained. Now the chest cavity is dry. One finger has discovered the source and stanched the flow. With his free hand he begins. From the periphery in toward his finger, he dissects in a circular pattern. Each snip of his scissors clears away more of the infected scar. Now and then a hidden sac of pus is exposed and wiped away. The superior vena cava appears. More camouflage is mowed. He closes in. All barriers to the truth are broken down until at last there is only his index finger emerging from a rent in the great vein whose wall, weakened by infection, had given way. Only the plug of his finger inside the vein prevents exsanguination. "Curved arterial clamp," he says. His voice is flat, calm. He fits the jaws of the clamp about his index finger, sits it down upon the wall of the vein about the gash; he withdraws his finger; there is a spurt of new blood, then the sound of the teeth of the clamp clicking into place, once, twice, three times, and the bleeding has stopped. All that remains is to stitch up the tear and release the clamp. Done, he swiftly removes the infected graft and replaces it with another. Looking over the shoulder of this surgeon, I see a faithfulness to vocation, a testimony to the exorbitant demands of two hearts—the patient's, heaving there within view, and his own.

Later, in the locker room we are drinking coffee.

"How do you do it?" I ask him.

"I just follow things as they are," he says. "There are always spaces between, where you can go."

There is no speck of irony in him. In this alone is he like a monk. But I think there was something besides vision and touch and memory at work here. Call it intuition, or a quality of the spirit. The senses have nothing to do with it. Had the lights gone out, he would have finished in the dark. He could be blind and deaf, I think, and have done it as well. There is a place where knowledge and technique stop and the spirit moves where it wants. The surgeon had better follow.

As with the monk his rosary, so with the surgeon his instruments; the handling of designated objects induces a feeling of tranquillity. But Wayne Flye does not attach a mystical significance to his work. For him it is the tangible that counts.

"You're good," I tell him. "That was close."

"Think so?" he smiles. "Nowadays the tools do it for you."

Days, nights, days, nights. So many hundreds of dark and light hours.

For some time I have been utterly depressed. Already the chant is becoming tiresome to me; all so patterned, divorced from humanity. It sounds about as vivacious as the strewing of ashes on a sidewalk. There is something of insanity in it. My room, which I had grown to love, seems bewitched, a bare tidy cell from which something essential has been banished. Its very tidiness disturbs. How can I be expected to find anything in a place so uncluttered, empty, really, as though all of the furnishings had been removed to prepare for a visit by the exterminator. I can find things only if they are left lying about in the open. It is the same with all these antique masterpieces. Saint George in love with the dragon; in love with his killing of the dragon, his flat face pale with spent lust rather than religious ecstasy. And the paintings of Tintoretto with which this house is smeared. A whole pantheon of gross, sexless indecencies in the name of Christ. All those pretty bodies devoid of honesty. They have no more to do with Christianity than I do. I do not see faith in them; everything depicted is so inert, remote. Two dozen beautiful youths draped upon crosses, with their clean bloodless wounds, their pale dry brows, their impeccably trimmed beards, their penislessness. I much prefer the German version with gouges running blood and runnels of sweat and skinny twisted legs. Perhaps it is the surgeon in me.

Even had I been among the faithful I should have eschewed icons. They are unnecessary, a hindrance, something between God and me that draws the eye to themselves.

I suppose the abbot's treatment of Lorenzo in the refectory has something to do with my frame of mind. And then there is Pietro. This morning at breakfast, the novice who was pouring coffee asked me shyly and in newly found English whether I would like milk and sugar. Delighted to be addressed by someone if only on this level, I accepted both despite the fact that I take my coffee straight. Another small door had opened. In the evening, this from Pietro:

"These monks are all so unspiritual. I would much prefer a stricter abbey. How sweet the life in the old monasteries must have been. This place is positively unedifying. If you don't watch them every minute, the novices do wicked things."

"Like what?"

"Speaking directly to guests, for one."

"Come now, Pietro, you're jealous over that novice asking me how I took my coffee. That's it, isn't it?"

"He knows the rules as well as I do. They are dumb Italians," he says. I am shocked.

"That is stupid," I tell him. "And furthermore, you are bored and boring." Hurt to the bone, he whisks himself from the room with a single stroke. An hour later he is back with a little bar of lavender soap that he had hidden away. But it won't do. More and more I see him as a rabid and afflicted soul, a born Inquisitor who sees sin in the least twitch of an eyelid. Therefore constant watchfulness is necessary, as though he alone were called to great tasks. Such a man places high value on the outer proofs of virtue—the downcast glance, the purity of the singing voice, all of that. He is the sort of priest who would convert with the sword, if need be. I see that, in an odd way, the abbot relies on his severity and worldliness. Why? But it is not just Pietro and the abbot. It is all this praying for the sake of praying. Do they really believe in the efficacy of their acts of prayer? Or are these simply rites that must be performed? Like chores in a garden? I imagine them praying the way a sheep grazes, on and on, without a pause, without a thought. More and more I see them as a tepid black coagulum flowing listlessly this way and that. But I am a guest here! Discretion, do not abandon me. Even to think such thoughts, much less write them down, is to act the asp in a basket of fig leaves.

"I'm going to Venice today," I tell Pietro.

"Will you be back for the evening meal?" asks Pietro.

"Absolutely not."

"Have a good time," he says. But I do not. From San Marco, the abbey is a hulk that has been blown in from the sea and all of whose sailors have been dead for years. Venice, which only yesterday had been a magic dream of beauty and so full of possibility, seems a giant cloaca, carved and frescoed over every millimeter, into which filth of all kinds is collected. What a sour, rankled old man I have become, a stateless person. By evening I am once again aboard the vaporetto laden with Grand Armagnac and a large box of chocolate creams. From the boat the facade of the monastery has caught the last pink. It seems to me at this moment to have captured its whole past, retained it somehow, and now to be reflecting it in a continuous even glow, the way ruins reveal to us their previous complete existence. To my mingled surprise and indignation, I find myself impatient to get there. I hurry to the refectory where the monks are standing each behind his place. They have just come from the choir and their habits are still singing the last notes of the chant. Later, I give Pietro a strudel I have bought for him. He carries on about it with unfeigned joy. Lickity-split! And it is gone, with the creature sighing and mopping his chops. It is moving to see how much of the world he loves and denies himself. Thrown into ecstasy by candy yesterday and strudel today. What purpose is served by the denial of strudel?

Up at dawn. In the cloister strolling off the night's lust. Then to the refectory for sweet strong coffee and the stale crusts they call toast. Then again to my room to begin a morning of writing. My life is as rhythmical and obscure as though it were being passed at the bottom of the lagoon. The weather has turned unaccountably sultry. I open the casements wide and let in the honeyed air of Venice. Directly ahead, in the lagoon, men in gondolas are poling in unison. They are not slim, but hefty, beefy, and they wear identical striped shirts and stocking caps. I assume that they are members of a team of athletes. There is a great delicacy in the way they handle the poles. It is more than mere strength. It is grace and precision as well.

I am drawn from my desk to the open window by a

frantic buzzing. The noise is made by two large dragonflies in the act of mating on the very ledge. How did they come there, so far from the least vegetation and fresh water? Never mind, their presence is no more strange than my own. They are tail to tail and glued, but now, it seems, full of second thoughts. All four wings row hard to break a terrible suction. The single crosshatched tube that is the fusion of their bodies bends as if to snap. Joined, they are a single lunatic insect in the throes and striving for separation. If this be sex, I'll have no more of it. At last, the wretched four-wings gives up its struggle, and taking off sideways, awkwardly settles for being airborne. It is like Achilles dragging off the body of Hector. One must beware of love. Like certain Bedouins, you can die of it.

To the park, then, since there is again to be no writing. I follow one of the gravel paths to a point where it intersects with two others. Lining the paths, ancient white capitals hung with marble grapes. Standing guard at the juncture, a large stone angel with wings half raised. Gabriel, at the very least, or Michael. On the pedestal a paste of droppings and feathers. So! Angels too molt; they defecate.

No sooner have I taken a seat on the bench than I hear the pebbles of the walk crunching beneath light footsteps. A quick scattering that identifies the maker long before he comes into view. "Dom Sebastiano," I call out. A moment later he is standing before me in the usual posture of humility—head bent forward, eyes lowered, as though feeling the weight of his sins. Of them all he is the only thin one, lean as Cassius. Of them all he alone conforms to my notion of the physiognomy of Christ—gaunt, sallow, his face harried, preoccupied. I can imagine this one reigning from the tree, surrounded by a golden nimbus. His movements have none of the heaviness of the other monks. He is quick and jerky. His fingers flicker, his head too. Even his habit is caught up in the commotion and trembles at the hem. When he raises his eyelids I see that his eyeballs bulge, showing altogether too much white. This gives him the expression of a horse skittering above a rattlesnake. His face is drained of color save for a swatch of bruise beneath each eye. Standing still, he seems to be containing himself by an effort of will lest his entire body break apart. In his company my own body speeds up, feeling the need to keep pace. What, I wonder, had he done before he entered the monastery? Often it was possible to guess. One of the monks had retained the slow clumsiness of a peasant farmer. Another, the impetuosity of a soldier. Still another, the grace and balance of a mariner. But here was someone who gave not the least sign of how or where he had lived before becoming a monk. Although he looks to be thirty years old, I know that it is quite possible that he is much older.

"Will you sit with me for a while?" I ask him. He blushes and picks at something that might have happened to his habit. Still, he does sit on the very edge of the bench, as though to spring to his feet at any moment.

The sun had come out; my first view of it in a week. Within minutes the days of damp and cold have evaporated. In his heavy woolen habit Sebastiano perspires frantically. His skin radiates heat.

"What do you wear in the summer?" I ask.

"This," he says, "the same thing."

"But it must be hot. You are wet all the time."

He smiles.

"The wool absorbs the sweat," he says. "I do not mind too much. Still, I prefer the cold."

I see that he does mind, a great deal, and that the summer months are hell for him.

"Where are you from, Sebastiano?"

"Tuscany. An old village. Monte San Savino. My family are farmers in the hills there."

"Have you always wanted to be a monk? Even as a child?"

"No, not always. I was a student at the university. But I studied too hard. Something happened to my mind. I could not pass the examinations. For a long time I could not think. Then God spoke to me and brought me here."

"Are you happy here?"

"Oh, very happy. I am a good monk. I place myself in God's hands. He will see that I am rescued."

"Rescued? From what?"

But he had already sprung from the bench and hurried away.

I awake feeling somewhat ill. My sides ache and I am coughing.

I should hate to become sick here. Since it is only death that they trust, I should be afraid that they would not take my flesh seriously, leave several stones unturned. Would their physical diffidence keep them from resuscitating me mouth-to-mouth or massaging my heart? I rather think they might gather round the bed and rejoice, as long ago the nuns did in the hospital in Troy, New York, where I followed my father on his hospital rounds. I remember them grouped like lamps in a darkened room, the face of the patient graying away, their own aglow with an imperturbable golden light. Not for me the festive air of the deathbed. No, thanks. I can wait for the wonders of eternity. Wrap me not in tranquil joy. A shot of penicillin will do just fine.

It is the morning of the next day. I am once again in the little park. The sound of gravel crunching leads me to where Sebastiano is pacing to and fro. I block his path with my body. He looks for all the world like a blackbird—raising one wing or unclasping a twig to some indeterminate purpose.

"What is it?" I ask him. "Something is wrong."

"It is nothing. Nothing. I am tired. Please let me pass." His face has the fatalism of a slave.

As we talk, he holds one hand at his chest to brace against some shortness of breath. Or to pry loose a stone.

"Tell me," I say.

"I cannot sleep. All night I toss and turn. In the morning I am tired. I come to the park to rest."

"Your appetite," I say. "I have watched you in the refectory. You eat as much as the others."

"You are not the one to criticize," he tries to smile. "You are already famous here for eating nothing."

"Never mind about me," I tell him. "You are thinner even than when I arrived." The man appears to be in a state of dread and exhaustion. I see him mounting his cot each night and riding it furiously toward dawn.

"Hold out your hands," I tell him, "and spread your fingers."

He does and I examine his palms, half expecting to find stigmata other than those of thyrotoxicosis. What a rage for the terrific I am developing here.

I tear a sheet from my notebook and lay it across his outstretched fingers. The paper vibrates, then falls to the ground.

"Look up," I say. Again he obeys. "Now down." The veined marble lids drop over the proptosed globes, leaving a rim of white sclera showing above the iris. I see that no matter in which direction he gazes his pupils are surrounded by white. The whites of his eyes are bloodshot. In the bright sunshine, he blinks and tears.

"Look here," I say, and with one quick movement reach up and pull down the front of his habit to expose his neck. Sebastiano is shocked.

"Please," he whispers. "I must go."

"I want to feel your neck," I say. What I am seeking is

there. A soft diffuse swelling that occupies the front of his neck. With one hand securing his shoulder, I bend to place my ear against that swelling. He jumps at the contact.

"Don't breathe," I say. "Hold your breath." He does and I hear the loud bruit of blood eddying there. Against my ear there comes the confirmatory thrill. For a long moment I hold him in the diagnostic embrace, listening to the malicious huff-puff of that hyperthyroid gland.

"It's called Graves' disease. Your thyroid gland is making too much hormone. It makes your body run too fast. That is the cause of your nervousness, your sleeplessness. There is a medicine. First you need to have a blood test to make sure."

"No, no," he says. "Dom Pietro is right. I am possessed. The abbot has seen these things before. He knows what to do."

Possessed! It is my turn to recoil under the force of a word.

"You are no such thing," I say. "You are sick and you need medicine. In a few days you will feel better. You will be able to sleep."

"No," he says. "When Padre Abate returns from Rome, we will have an exorcism."

"That is crazy," I say. "Where do you find an exorcist around here?"

"Dom Paolo is an exorcist. He will do it."

Paolo! The portly old choirmaster, with his music teacher's gold-rimmed glasses. I try to imagine him, masseters clenched about a hiss of incantation, habit hitched, cincture tightened. Now he takes up the silver crucifix and advances upon the devil . . .

"But you must take the medicine. If I am wrong, it will not hurt you to take it for a few days. If I am right, you will be much better. What do you say?"

"No. I must go. Let me pass."

"This afternoon I go to Venice. I return with the medicine."

"No." And he breaks free from my grasp and is gone. A gull flies overhead, its testy scream long outlasting the shadow of its flight upon the footpath.

I am in my room waiting for the inevitability of Pietro. He comes.

"What's the big idea of telling Sebastiano that he is possessed? He is suffering from hyperthyroidism. He bears all the stigmata of it." I list them. "The rapid pulse, the bulging eyes, the voracious appetite accompanied by weight loss, the fine tremor, the intolerance to heat, the unrelenting anxiety."

"You examined him?"

"I certainly did."

"That was an infraction. Padre Abate will be angry." Pietro himself is furious.

"Say what you will, I'm off to Venice for the medicine."

"You have no understanding of our lives. Perhaps if you would kneel and pray . . ."

"I am less a kneeler than a bower down who keeps the stones of this earth close in his vision. Besides, there are my pagan arthritic knees."

But he is not to be disarmed. He spins and sweeps toward the door, sending his habit from his ankles with cold grace.

"I'll take the matter to the abbot," I say.

"Padre Abate is in Rome for three days. He has other duties, you see."

"I'm not waiting."

"The exorcism has been planned for some time. Sebastiano desires it. The abbot has delayed only because he has felt that Sebastiano is not strong enough for the ordeal. It is to be performed upon Padre's return from Rome."

"Sebastiano needs propylthiouracil," I call after him.

For the hundredth time I try to decide why I have come here. I might as well have spent a month among cannibals. I am determined to treat Sebastiano, although it will mean that I must leave San Giorgio. What it will mean for Sebastiano beyond regaining his health, I have no idea. I suppose I should care more about that. He will have broken his vows of obedience. Perhaps they will cast him out. The thought chills me. He belongs here most emphatically.

I have it. Enough for two weeks and the promise of a continued supply of the medicine. It took less than I anticipated. A few phone calls, the word *Yale,* the other word *professor.* Such syllables in Italy have a magical incantatory power of their own. I find Sebastiano in the laundry to which he has been presently assigned.

"Here." I press the bottle of pills into his hand. "Take one four times every day at regular intervals. And don't skip."

"No," he says. "I cannot."

"You fool! Take it or go to Hell!" I am shocked by my outburst. It matters much more than I thought. I must have this . . . this evidence.

He is hesitant, reluctant. But the bottle is in his hand.

"It is not permitted," he says, but now without conviction. I have him.

"Listen, Sebastiano. Listen to me. I shall explain it all to Padre Abate upon his return. He is a kind and reasonable man. He loves you. How happy he will be to find you better. For two weeks only. If you are not improved, then go ahead with the exorcism. I'm dying to see one anyway. In the meantime, if I were you, I would not try to pray. It is too exhausting for you."

"Not pray?" The wild eyeballs threaten to pop their sockets. A day without prayer is a day lost. How does one talk to these aliens? Their citizenship is elsewhere. But I have him. I can tell by the glance he gives to the pills. It is the glance of a man looking at a food strange to him and wondering what it will taste like. If this works, I shall know why it was that I came here.

Back in time for Vespers. The church already dark. Why is it that night falls faster in a church than anywhere else? And is more absolute? More than night is falling here. I push open the side door, but for a moment the darkness will not let me in. I press against it, but it has no give where I am concerned. There is no floor in it. It is bottomless. I advance one foot, toeing for a hold. Within, I stand quite near the choir, yet hidden from them in a small alcove. In a moment the monks file across my path, close enough so that I can see them in the candlelight. They open their mouths as one, and now come those phrases and strains that, even as I listen, leave the realm of music and direct themselves toward what I presume to call the soul. It is not so much voice as echo.

Right smack in the middle of Vespers, from out in the courtyard, Dom Cat breaks his vow of silence and begins to yowl. Forced, desperate cries of sexual desolation that begin low in the throat, then rise quickly to the soprano range. It is like the whine of a chain saw moving through a plank of oak. For a moment the chant falters, then gathers itself. Do I imagine a streak of repressed desire among the silver monotony? On and on the creature howls for all the rest of us, the reservoir of lust of seventeen men, overflowing. Nor does he stop with the end of the chant but continues to spray the night with his rage until eventual sleep deafens us.

"What in the world . . . ?" I ask Dom Pietro in the morning.

"The devil," he smiles.

"Oh, good," I say. "We may yet have an exorcism."
Once again Pietro warns me not to interfere.
"It is none of your affair," he says again. "You do not understand us. . . ."

Now I must leave the Abbey of San Giorgio. It is not mere work that I am forbidden; it is my work—that respectful interference in the lives of others that constitutes the diagnosis and treatment of disease. I simply cannot remain here to watch a man with thyrotoxicosis exorcised for demons. Here, among the kidnapped, the never-set-free. Strange black flowers they are that cannot live in the sunlight. Plucked and laid upon an altar. I suppose what bothers me most about them is that they lack scope. These decades of stagnation have made them unfit for the company of man. How they wrong themselves by refusing to be part of their own age, neglecting what exists now. Assuming the existence of God, the monk is possessed of Him in exact proportion as he is dispossessed of everything else. Dom Pietro is right. I do not understand it. Not at all.

It was a mistake to come here. Were I ever to express my belief in God it would be a courteous salute into the distance, and smartly delivered rather than this groveling in a reliquary where men do not tend their aging parents, or carry the burdens of others, or accept the honest concern of infidels. In one hour, I leave for Venice for more propylthiouracil. If I have to cram it down his throat.

On the way back from San Marco I struggle against the possessive motion of the vaporetto, the monotonous shuddering of the boat demanding from me an admission of contentment. And I *am* happy to be returning to the abbey. Going home, I think, and the idea takes me by surprise. To be receptive; to wait, that is all. But then comes evening. And with it, the lamps of doubt. What is it that in this hushed house, in these hushed hours, draws near? Then recedes? There! It comes again. Circling and circling, pausing, darting away.

Padre Abate has returned from Rome. Within an hour I am summoned to his presence. The change in his manner from benevolent warmth to icy shuddering rage stuns me. He himself looks sick with displeasure, his face gray, sweating. Is this difficult for him too? I begin, knowing that it is hopeless.

"I hope that you have had a pleasant trip. By now you know of my treatment of Sebastiano. You will be pleased to learn that he is already much improved. He is calmer; he is sleeping well."

"It is the infirmarian's duty to look after our health." His voice is terrible, frigid.

"Then I am happy to have been able to assist him in this."

"I did not give you permission to work here, nor Sebastiano permission to accept your ministrations. It was wrong of you to do this, wrong of him to accept. You have violated our rule." All at once I am like a child who is being scolded for having misbehaved. To my astonishment tears of humiliation spring to my eyes. Why should I care what he thinks of me? I am not one of his monks. But I do care.

"You are overtired, Padre Abate. You yourself look unwell. The rigors of your journey, and now this . . ."

He glances up.

"Your diagnoses are presumptuous. Perhaps it would be best for you to leave the Abbey of San Giorgio."

"And Sebastiano?" I ask.

"That is none of your affair."

My temper flares. "It was not his fault. I forced him to comply. You simply cannot bear that such a benefice be delivered by an infidel. That's it, isn't it?"

With a small nod, I am dismissed.

I have packed my bags and stacked them near the door of my room. Now I stand at the window inhaling for the last time the honeyed mist of Venice. I cannot wait to get out of here. *Precipitatamente. Hic et nunc.* First vaporetto in the morning. Of all the things I could have done in Italy, I had to come to this dismal monastery and get thrown out to boot. Take care, God. If the gift of prophecy has not deserted me, you dwell in the last of your houses. Your days are numbered. These sixteen relics are your only worshippers left. Soon you will exist solely in paintings and statues, nothing but the work of art you were always meant to be.

It is nine o'clock in the evening. Time for *Riposo e Silenzio.* Twenty doors are shut, twenty bolts shot. Grate, clang, thump, click . . . and the monks are through for the day.

Toward midnight I am startled by a knock at the door. Pietro, I think. He is the last person I want to see.

"Go away," I call out.

A pause and then another knock. That would not be Pietro. He would have barged in. I open the door to see old Lorenzo. He is plainly distraught.

"What is it, Lorenzo?"

"It is Padre Abate. He is very sick. Will you come?"

"I am not permitted. In any case, I am leaving here in the morning."

The old monk takes me by the hand and tries to draw me toward the door.

"What is the matter with him?"

"You will come?" I follow Lorenzo down the long dark corridors and through doors leading into the living quarters from which until now I have been forbidden. The infirmarian opens the door and steps aside. The room is tiny and painfully neat, devoid of depth and looking like something flat that has been stretched on a frame. It is without wrinkles, webs or laps. To step into it is to lose a dimension. The small armoire, open, is bare save for a few black socks, a short pile of white linen and one black habit. On a writing table, several books, pen and paper; on the walls, a wooden crucifix, and, set in black velvet and framed, a bit of yellow bone. Under it, the legend: RELIC OF ST. BENEDICT (VERIFIED). But who shall say where sentiment may not exist?

The abbot is neither sitting in his chair nor standing to receive me, but is lying facedown upon his cot. Nor does he turn his head to glance in my direction. The infirmarian lowers a blanket to the abbot's waist. There, bristling between his shoulder blades I see a huge abscess. It has been present for weeks, I am certain. The area of inflammation is fully ten centimeters in diameter with bubbles of pus issuing from multiple sites of drainage in the already gangrenous skin. The mass crepitates beneath my palpating fingers. A gas-producing clostridium? The man's skin is hot, his breathing comes in short little gasps. He seems in a profound lethargy, yet is fully awake, I know it. Solemnity issues forth from his already perished flesh.

So, I think, His Augustitude hath contracted a boil!

"It is a carbuncle," I say. "It needs to be lanced. Now." Neither man makes any reply.

"Show me what you have," I say to Lorenzo. We go to the infirmary. I look over the meager equipment on his shelf. There is only unsterile cotton, a small bottle of what looks and smells like Mercurochrome and an antique scalpel with MADE IN GERMANY carved into the handle.

"Do you have such a thing as a local anesthetic? Novocaine?" Lorenzo is mystified.

"Bake the cotton in the oven for twenty minutes. First wrap it in paper," I tell the old man. I take up the bistoury and test it for sharpness. It is hopelessly dull. I shall have to whet it. I find a pumice stone used by the infirmarian to abrade calluses and a cruet of olive oil. Half an hour of circular honing, and the knife is usable. Barely. We boil it in water for ten minutes and return to the abbot's cell. He has not moved in our absence. His body has a deflated look as though the voluminous flesh has slipped from his bones and he has already begun to sink in. A light, greenish phosphorescence, the emanation of decay, shines from his cavernous skull. For a moment I think he is dead. But then he breathes.

"There is no anesthetic," I say. "I will apply ice to reduce the pain of the incision, but it will hurt. I must make two cuts, a cruciate incision so that it will stay open." Silence. I hold the ice to the surface of the boil, then pour the contents of the bottle over the lesion.

"Now," I say. And think to myself, don't scream. I am praying silently for him not to. I want him to succeed. I cut. And the man on the cot howls—a cascade of vowels that bounce back from the high ceiling. I steel myself against the sound and draw the knife along the fiery mound for its full length. Because it is dull, I must press firmly. Again, in the same track, a third time. Midway through the third stroke a wave of foul-smelling greenish pus lifts from the cut and runs across the back of the man. My hands are warm and wet with it. All the while the abbot cries out; his body is wracked with sobs. Now for the second incision. I reach around with my left hand and clamp it over his mouth.

"Shhhh. The others will hear and be frightened," I whisper. And I cut. The force of his cry bursts through the slats of my fingers. But what comes out is only the snorting of a horse. Gentle pressure expresses a great amount of putrefaction. Lorenzo gasps and crosses himself as the stream continues for minutes. When, at last, the flow has dwindled, I insert a twisted wick of the cotton into the wound to hold it open. I cover the place with a small towel.

"*Ti calma*," I say. "It is done. *Respira forte*." It seems right to use Italian. "Soon you will feel better. Already, the pain is not so severe?" For the first time he raises his head and nods slightly.

"Stay with him. I will be back in one hour."

In my room I find three of my shirts washed and neatly folded on the precisely turned-down bed. That Pietro! I scrub the dried corruption from my hands and pour a glass of brandy. The hot ribbon of liquor winds down through me. I pour a second, and carry it with me down-stairs to the side door of the church. To my surprise it is morning. The sunlight streaming through the high dome picks out each facet and edge, defining, washing, coloring the stone. I sit, listening to the whole island beating like a heart, and I sip the brandy.

Did he think he would vanquish pain merely by being one of the serene elect? Arrogance. Or was it a trial he had set for himself out of pride and obstinancy? And oh that bellowing, that terrible yowling, as though something, a passion which had been contained for a lifetime, had broken free. The whole biography of the man had been written in that single episode when, for the first time, derobed of his habit he wore the genuine lineaments of suffering man-kind. Had he not sent for me, had he chosen instead to die, he would have done so in the full understanding of why he had lived. But he was afraid. Now it is too late.

It is time to visit the abbot. He is sitting on the edge of the cot. I hardly know him. His face is white as a gardenia. In spite of his bulkiness, he is strangely diaphanous. All of his features have relaxed, "given" in a way, even his shoulders and spinal column—crumpled. He seems shorter, rounder. Nor is this pitiable to behold, but rather a change toward the human, the harmonious. This man, I think, will be henceforward incapable of silencing the laughter of monks with a pair of chilly *piano*s.

I accept the seat offered by his gesture and wait for him to speak.

"Do you know that I am from peasant stock?" he says at last. "My family are farmers from the hills around Como. I am one of nine children. We were very poor." I feel obliged to respond.

"To be born ignobly is a lesser misfortune than to live so."

The abbot smiles.

"In any case," I say, "let me change your dressing. Then you must rest. Lorenzo will bring you food."

I go to stand behind him, help him to lift the habit from his back, and gently push him forward. The towel is stuck to his back by the dried effusion. I pick out the cotton. It is chased by a slide of new purulence. But the swelling and redness have begun to subside. The lips of the incision remain widely open allowing for drainage.

"Warm compresses, now," I tell Lorenzo. "And Sebastiano?" The abbot nods.

Outside the door, a wave of elation. I can stay! I can stay!

The others of course had heard. That passionate bellowing, those howled vowels that had been contained all his life and only now had gathered from somewhere deep within and flung themselves into the farthest reaches of his abbey, to the cells of his monks where they lay in their beds and trembled.

"Did you really cut into him?" Pietro asks. Before I can answer he covers his eyes and shudders. "No, don't tell me."

"There are few things I can count on in this world," I say. "The squeamishness of the religious is one of them."

"Speaking for the community, we are grateful for what you have done for our beloved Padre." He says this with precision. Elocuting, really.

With the lancing of the boil comes an unexpected benefice. Pietro spells it out for me.

"Padre Abate wishes me to tell you that in the time immediately following *Compieta* and prior to *Riposo e Silenzio*, the older monks, two or three at a time, may visit with you for dialogue. This is to continue for as long as you wish it during the remainder of your stay with us, which the abbot hopes will be lengthy. It is the expectation of the abbot that the community, excepting the novices, of course, will make your further acquaintance through these conversations. In the interest of uniformity he suggests that these visits take place here in the guest room." It is apparent from his tone that Pietro is resentful. The message is delivered with ill-concealed distaste. I do not try to hide my own elation.

"Personally," says Pietro, "I doubt any good will come of it. Some of them are really rather dumb Italians." I am shocked at this second slip of bigotry.

"Listen, Pietro . . ."

"It goes without saying that you are to keep in mind at all times the holiness of this house."

"Did the abbot tell you to say that?" By his silence I know that he did not. Pietro is jealous.

"Come tonight, then, and bring Lorenzo and Antonio."

"Lorenzo! Holy Mother of the Word Incarnate!" He leaves. My plan is to loosen their tongues with brandy, ravish them with chocolate creams. And ply them with questions.

The first to arrive is Lorenzo, scarcely five feet tall, a cap of cropped white hair over an unmarked face. He has been in the monastery for sixty years. I pour him a glass of brandy.

"Un biccierino?"

"Mille grazie." The others arrive. Antonio, with whom

I have never exchanged a word, and instead of Pietro, Vittorio, the holy novice master. The sounds we must make to converse cause us to smile. They are a mixture of Italian, French, German and English. Even Latin is made use of *in extremis*. It is the Tower of Babel all over again. Yet somehow there is comprehension. It is an understanding beyond grammar and accent. Soon it is all wickedness, *chez moi*. Glass is clinked, a cigarette is lit, a chocolate cream is popped and with it ecstasy oozes across a long uncandied face. The temperature of the room rises. Now and then there is wafted to me the smell of ripe monk. Come to think of it, I have seen no other bathtubs save my own Gethsemanic appliance.

"Where do you bathe?" I ask.

They laugh happily but do not reply. About this, I see, I am to remain ignorant.

"What brought you here?" I ask Antonio.

"I love God," he says. A moment later I hear him say with the exact same intensity, "I love chocolate creams." The flesh of none of them, I suspect, is entirely dead. They all have much work to do. An hour later, they leave. The last to go is Lorenzo, plump as a pincushion and with many more colors in his face than when he arrived. Antonio, too, might be expected at this moment to be as besotted with wine as he is with Christ. It has been a lovely evening.

Now, each night, there is company. With what eagerness I wait for the sound of their soft knocking at my door. I have taken to leaving it ajar so that I can spy on them as they approach. Clotheslines have been strung the length of the corridor leading to my room. Sheets, pillowcases, underwear, handkerchiefs and socks are hung there. The monks must part the laundry with the backs of their hands as though it were beaded curtains. Dom Paolo, the choir-

master-cum-exorcist, comes each night. He, it seems, is to
be my sparring partner; he will guard the others against
contamination from my worldliness. This is the way we
speak:

"Where are you buried?" I ask him.

"In the crypt beneath the floor. You see how convenient
it is? We simply disappear into the premises. There is nothing for the world to dispose of. Just so do we become our
beloved abbey."

"How old were you when you entered this monastery?"

"I was ten, but long before that, I knew that I was to
be given to God, that I must learn not to trifle. But we do
not any longer take in children. It is thought wiser to let
them have a taste of the world first."

I disagree. I tell him, "I think it more natural and wiser
to enter as a child before having been seized by life. At
least it would forgo the need for painful renunciation. Or
later, perhaps, much later in life, after a series of failures.
Then it would seem a blessed haven."

"You quite misunderstand the monastic urge," he says.
"And the concept of the *formation* of a monk."

"What if one of you gets appendicitis?"

"We are very healthy."

"But appendicitis, after all."

"Ah well, you see that we have not." Then, as an af-
terthought: "We place ourselves in the hands of Christ."

"You are more severe than your predecessors who lived
here seven centuries ago. They, at least, were open to medicine. Even that delivered to them by infidels from the
East."

"You live among us like an angel," says Vittorio.

"More like a ghost," I say. "Or a bumblebee visiting a

secret garden. I should much prefer to do some work. But Padre Abate will not permit it."

"The abbot knows best."

"Well, then, if I am to be an angel, I shall put my head under my wing and think of nothing."

"Ah, there you are, Dom Lorenzo," I say. "Today I caught you sleeping at your orisons." He blushes; the others laugh gently. *"Dolci?"* I pour him a large brandy. He has brought me a postcard upon which is a photograph of San Giorgio from the other side of the lagoon. He points to a dot which is the window of this very room. I *am* thrilled. I listen as he tells the others once again that I saved the abbot's life.

"Once," says Paolo, "not so very long ago, when one of us died, Dom Tommaso, a very holy man"—he looks at the others; they nod in agreement—"when we went to prepare his body for the crypt, we saw that he still wore the cincture about his waist. So tightly had he drawn it that it had bitten into him. The flesh had grown over it."

I make no reply to this.

"But we no longer tighten the cincture." He sighs at the passing of a happier time.

"How do you support yourselves?"

"We are not a mendicant order. Only if someone wishes to give us a gift."

"I see." And make a mental note.

"Who decides which duties each of you is to perform? The refectory, for instance?"

"Each of us must serve a turn at kitchen and table."

"Pietro says he hates it," I betray shamelessly. Then hurry on.

• • •

Within days, the debate peters out and like true companions we fall to telling stories. Vittorio tells a story about Saint Euphemia whose church is the oldest in Venice. The others know the story and give encouraging nods.

"Not long ago," he begins, with the air of someone who has invented a new sauce, "it was discovered that the church was in danger of collapsing. Workmen were called in to shore up and reinforce the structure. During the digging, the shovel of one of the workmen struck a hard object buried beneath the foundation of the church. The object was uncovered and found to be the coffin of none other than Saint Euphemia herself. The shovel had broken the ancient wood of the box and had stuck the still undisintegrated head in the nose. From the wound thus caused, fresh blood flowed." Vittorio's eyes blaze at the thought of the miracle. Yet he speaks of it as though it were an ordinary event, something expected.

"It was in all of the newspapers," he says.

"Really?" I say. There is no irony here. Only my presence among them is ironic.

"Padre Abate," I begin, "told me today that Ezra Pound used to visit him often here. Do you know that Pound was a Fascist, a bigot and a traitor to his country?"

"But you did not know," Paolo exonerates, "that Ezra Pound was hung up in a cage by the American soldiers in Pisa? When he died, the body was placed in a gondola and poled away. How sad it was. He was not a bad, bad man. His funeral, how desolate, the lone gondola disappearing from the island, bearing only the body, *solo, abbandonato.*"

All through these evenings, Pietro remains silent. I think he is sulking. Only now and then, like a diva who cannot bear to leave the stage, he makes his bit of noise in the wings.

"Why is it that you do not pray?" This from Vittorio, the holy.

"These buildings say my prayers for me; I don't have to. Besides, I have bony spurs on my knees. Exostoses, they are called. It hurts to kneel. See?" I pull up my pants to show him.

"Then you must kneel and offer it up," says Paolo, barely glancing.

"Easy for you to say, Dom Paolo. Raised out of this world, you feel no pain in knee or back."

"We do feel it," he replies. "It is an opportunity for virtue."

"What possible virtue can there be in pain? Remember, I am a doctor."

"To do penance is virtuous. The path to God is hard and rugged."

"Yes," I say. "I see that it is."

"I saw that you did not finish your plate again tonight."

"Oh, that."

Outside the room the mist gathers. Soon there will be rain. Although they do not know, tonight is to be the last of it. I have told Padre Abate of my departure. I wish only to make them smile one last time. I point to the crucifix crusted with amethyst.

"Do you know why the stone is purple?" I ask and go on. "One day Bacchus, the god of wine, angry over some imagined slight or a falling-off of worshippers, swore that the very next human being he saw would be devoured by the tigers that ran always at his side. Just then a beautiful innocent young girl happened by. The tigers leaped. At that instant, the girl cried out to the goddess Athena for help. Athena took pity on the girl and instantly turned her into a pillar of pure white stone. Now when Bacchus saw what he had caused, he was filled with remorse, and in atonement he poured over it the juice of his sacred grapes. And that, my dear, dear friends, is how the amethyst came to be purple." They are enchanted, the way children are enchanted by a story. We all have another brandy; there are more *buona sera*s than in the last act of *The Barber of Seville*.

When they have gone, I open the windows and the rain rushes in. Here and there the lagoon leaps up to grab the fresh drops, zealous to convert them to salinity.

Tomorrow evening I shall leave San Giorgio. It is no less painful to leave than it would be to stay. Exile simply cannot be the proper condition of man. Heaven is for the heavenly, and I am not one of those, each of whom is like a river that leaves behind its name and shape, the whole course of its path, to vanish into the vast sea of God. I cannot do that. I love my name which was my father's name, and the name of my children. I am proud of my few accomplishments, ashamed of my many failures; there are human beings I would die for. And so I depart this antechamber of the hereafter where faith is like a fierce orange cat who might claw the one who reaches out or settle to its belly and purr. You never know. Winning faith is like trying to tame a wild animal. One can try too hard. A little coyness is better.

Pietro feeds ravenously off me.

"Stay," he pleads. "Stay if you want to. For as long as you want. Where will you go?"

"To Florence, and then home."

"Florence! Such a long train ride; it will be crowded, noisy. What is there in Florence that we do not have here? You must go to Torcello, the other islands here in the bay of Venice. You have not met the Armenian fathers at San Lorenzo. Byron studied there, you know."

O my batch of monks! Shall we ever meet again? Not

here, I think. Perhaps in the plains of air. For I shall not return. Already it seems to me that the Isola di San Giorgio does not exist except as the island within myself, that isolated interior place upon which for a brief time I was marooned, and whose every corner I searched for the illumination of faith, and failed. I have not learned to pray. The closest I have come to praying is to ask this island to reveal the secrets it knows. But no building has the power to change a man's soul or produce a Sabbath of the heart. Still, still, I have become simpler. I shall no longer question or ask for proof. The fact remains that I can only find happiness in human love. The love of God won't do.

Perhaps I should not have come. But there was no way to avoid it. I had come, I suppose, seeking someone who possessed the key to something which all my life had been a mystery to me. Someone human, yet who had risen above his humanity. I did not find him here. Now I go back to my life. I shall practice no rites, say no prayers. Instead I shall permit myself superstition. It is simpler than religion and has not the burden of morality. I shall continue to make sacrifices to urban and forest deities, believing as I do that symbolic gestures enhance the sense of oneness with all of nature. I shall go on doctoring lest I be tempted to lie down and cherish my sorrows. I shall watch the birds. I shall content myself with a few nuggets of laughter and memory. And I shall try to find human beings to hold in my arms. I am skeptical of great notions such as Mankind or God. It is nature that I love and man.

Padre Abate and I sit together in my room on the eve of my departure. It is the first time he has come. I offer him a glass of brandy.

"Grand Armagnac," I tell him.

"I know," he smiles. "I have been told. I have wanted to taste it for a long time." We sip for a minute in silence.

"Speaking metaphorically . . ." he begins and hesitates.
"That is always the best way, Padre Abate."
". . . I should say that what you let out of my body was the putrefaction of pride. I am all the more grateful."
"I long ago learned not to minimize the ailments of my patients. To the boiled, his boil is the worst boil in the whole history of boilage, his lancing the most painful and dangerous. Still, Padre Abate, it was just a boil. I have seen many like it. It is hardly worth the myth of martyrdom."
I am talking too much, too cleverly.
"Your mockery, too, is incisive. But I shall hold to my metaphor, if you don't mind. It serves me well."
I do not answer for it occurs to me that while I have played, often recklessly, with everything in life, this man does not play with his faith. He cannot afford to. I pour more brandy.
"I told you once," he says, "that the reason for your coming had not yet been revealed to me."
"And?"
He rises and walks to the window, and with one hand opens first one, then the other casement.
"Air and light pass through a window in both directions," he says and turns to leave. I rise to face him. He holds out his hand. I take it and bend to kiss his ring. But before my lips can touch the stone, he turns his hand, grasping mine in a candid American handshake. The convent does not exist in the world into which human love cannot force an entrance.

It is sunset. The community gathers on the terrace. Only the abbot is missing. No one speaks, as though we had vowed. Paolo holds my suitcase which he does not set down; Sebastiano, the typewriter; Lorenzo, the briefcase. The vaporetto, famous for its punctuality, is late. Why doesn't it come? I implore it to come. The waiting is too hard, too hard. At last, it thumps against the pier. "San Giorgio!" calls out the boatman. The suitcase is handed aboard, then the rest. *"Arrivederci.* Good-bye, good-bye. *Ciao. Ci vediamo."* Fifteen hands are clasped.

I do not look back until the boat is well into the lagoon. At last, I must. I turn to see them on the terrace gazing after me, swaying on the stems of their bodies as though their souls were stirring. They are grouped together, all except for Pietro who stands a little apart, erect, his habit billowing, stealing the last scene. Of them all it is he for whom my departure is hardest. Even so, I have to smile. If Isola di San Giorgio were to sink into the lagoon and the order came to evacuate, it would be Pietro and Pietro alone who would remain to die with his beloved abbey, black and erect upon the steps of the church, an exclamation point dissolving into the flood.

All at once, the sun sinks behind Venice and, as it does, for one precise moment the final rays strike the facade of the monastery, turning it red. Every window is filled with flames. The whole of the abbey is a crucible. Every window burning. Except one. Mine! And that one is black as night. It is the window which the abbot flung open in his dramatic act of ventilation and which I had forgotten to close. *I had broken a rule.*

Months later I shall wonder, and try to remember, what it was I felt then. Relief that I had made my escape through that black hole, or regret that I had gone from that holy house, every detail of which lies buried forever at the back of my eyes.

Fetishes

There is Audrey. And there is Leonard. Audrey had waited until she was thirty-two to marry. Not by choice; no one had asked her. But all the time she had never given up hope. so that when Leonard Blakeslee had come along, she had at once reached out her hands for him as though he were an exotic foreign dish whose very strangeness captured her appetite completely. "You'll love me?" she asked him, and never once in all these years had he given her reason to doubt it. The fact that no children had come along was briefly regretted by both of them, then accepted. Somehow, it suited them.

Leonard is an anthropologist. Every so often he goes off to New Guinea on an expedition among the Asmat. It is the only time they are separated. When he is away Audrey feels only half intact, bisected. And Leonard too, as he wrote in a letter (she has saved them all), is "never done with wanting you at my side, where you ought always to be, my darling." She loved that "ought always to be." It was courtly. When he is not going on in that vein, his letters are anthropological, having to do with the language of the tribe for which he is compiling a dictionary, the artifacts he is collecting, the myths and mores of the people, all of which Audrey reads with affection and even genuine interest. Leonard and his artifacts, she would say to her sister, Violet, with an indulgent smile. Not that Audrey is beautiful. No one but Leonard could accuse her of that. But what she had she had and that was the true love of her husband.

Another thing Audrey has right now is a ten-centimeter cyst on her right ovary which the doctors can't say for certain is benign, and so it will have to come out. Thank heavens Leonard isn't off on one of his expeditions, she thought.

Fifteen years ago, she had been forty-two then, every one of her upper teeth had been extracted while Leonard was in New Guinea. Pyorrhea, the dentist had said. Said it severely. "You've let it go. They are all rotten and ready to fall out on their own."

Audrey was flabbergasted. "I have to think," she had said. "My husband isn't here. He's in New Guinea." She remembered the man's contemptuous little smile. On the way home, she said to Vi, "But . . . Leonard . . ."

"Leonard is not a dentist," said Violet.

And so a few days later Audrey had gone through with it. She hadn't been out of that dentist's office ten minutes when she knew that she had made a dreadful mistake. Vi drove her home afterward. Lying down on the backseat of the car, her mouth numb, her cheeks stuffed with pledgets of cotton, she wondered what Leonard would think, how he would feel. And she recalled something she had heard him say to one of his students, she couldn't remember why: "No one," Leonard had said to the student, "can take your dignity away from you; you might throw it away yourself, but no one can take it away from you." Then and there Audrey decided that Leonard didn't have to know.

"You all right?" Vi asked from behind the wheel, and turned round to see at every red light.

Right from the start, Audrey had refused to take the denture out of her mouth, no matter the pain. There were dark blisters on her gums; she lisped. But she was determined. Leonard would be coming home in two months. Audrey persevered so that with weeks to spare, she had gotten used to the "prosthesis," as they called it, incorporated it. It had become second nature.

Oh, she had had to steel herself against the first times it had to come out, be cleaned, then reinserted. But she had surprised herself. She was calm, curious, even, as she turned it over in her hand, examining. Like a pink horseshoe, she decided, and how wise she was to have avoided the vulgarity of pure white. Ivory was more natural. Ivory has endured; ivory has kept faith. In time her palate had molded itself to fit, her gums were snug and secure in the hollow trough. Never, never would she remove her teeth anywhere but in a locked bathroom. She would keep them in at night. It was a myth that you had to take your dentures out at night. Before long, she had no qualms, didn't mind at all. The denture had become for her a kind of emblem of personal dignity, like one of those Asmat artifacts with magic properties, but this having to do with the one thing that mattered most to Audrey: Leonard. "It isn't really cheating," she told Violet.

"You're lucky," said Vi. "You're one of those people who don't show their teeth when they smile."

When at last Leonard burst into the room, gathered her in his arms and kissed her, she smiled as much from triumph as with happiness. "You never cease to charm me," he had said, and she knew then that she had done it. Leonard would never know.

But now it was fifteen years later. "Total abdominal

hysterectomy," the surgeon announced. "A clean sweep."
As though she were a kitchen floor! "What does that in-
clude?" she asked him. "The uterus, both ovaries, both
tubes," he told her. "Why my uterus?" She insisted upon
the personal pronoun. "Why my left ovary? My tubes?"
He then explained, rather too patiently, she thought, that
she didn't need her reproductive organs anymore, that the
risk of getting cancer in one of those organs was "not
inconsiderable." Human beings do not talk like that, she
thought. That is not human speech. "And," the surgeon
went on, "as long as we are going to be in there anyway . . ."
In there! Audrey could not keep her hand from passing
lightly across her abdomen. Then he spoke about the small
additional risk of the larger operation, said it was "negli-
gible." But Audrey already knew what it was to go through
life missing something. She wished fervently that she had
been able to keep her cyst a secret, like her teeth. You
would think it would be easier since the ovaries were inside
and safely hidden. Imagine having to carry them in a bag
between your legs, like testicles. And as for the risk of
getting cancer . . . is that a reason to have your organs
taken out? All of life is a risk. Living in California is a risk;
there might be an earthquake. First, her teeth, and now
her . . . her womanhood, yes, it was nothing short of that.
All at once the operation seemed part of a plot to take her
body apart. And she remembered the clink of coins years
ago, as that dentist stirred the change in his pocket, stirred
it on and on, enjoying the sound of it before he took up
the syringe and injected her with novocaine.

On the wall in back of the surgeon's desk was a colored
diagram of the female organs. Altogether, it resembled a
sweet-faced cow's head rising to the gentle curve of the
horns.

"No," she said, closing down. "No, that cannot be. Only
my ovary, the one with the cyst. Nothing else, unless there

is cancer." She would sign permission only for that. In the end, she had capitulated. "You're doing the right thing, I assure you, Mrs. Blakeslee," said the surgeon as she signed the permission sheet.

At the hospital, Leonard and Audrey followed the nurse into the room. "Get undressed and into this." The nurse held up a knee-length shirt open at the back. She did and over it put on the pale green brocade bed jacket Leonard had given her the night before. It had been arranged that Leonard was to wait in the solarium outside the operating rooms. The surgeon would talk to him there, let him know what he had found. Afterward, he would wait for Audrey to be wheeled down from the recovery room a few hours later.

"Visiting hours are over," commanded the page operator. "Will all visitors please leave now."

"Good luck," said Leonard with a smile that was much too bright for him. He's frightened, she thought, and felt tears filming her eyes. After Leonard had left, Audrey lay on the bed, thinking of him—the silky feel of the black hairs on his forearms, his smell of permanence, the sound of his singing. Leonard sang bass. It was her favorite. At sixty-one, his voice was as rich as ever. Sometimes, listening in church to that submarine vibrato, she would have moments of unecclesiastical commotion. Once, when she confessed it, Leonard reproached her with a waggle of his finger. Ah, but his was a magic throat.

"I'm Dr. Dowling." The man had knocked and come in at the same time. It is what happens in hospitals, she thought. She was glad to be wearing the green bed jacket. So long as she had it on, there was protection.

"The anesthesiologist," he explained. "I'll be putting you to sleep tomorrow. Any questions?"

Audrey shook her head. He had an important sort of

face, florid, with jowls made even more congressional by the white political hair that escaped from beneath his green surgical cap. He was wearing a scrub suit of the same color and, over that, a white laboratory coat. The strings of a mask dangled.

"Open your mouth wide as you can." He peered in.

"I see you have an upper plate. Out it comes in the morning before you leave this room. The nurse will mind it for you."

Mute shadows of words trembled at her lips.

"But I never take it out, only to clean . . ."

"Well, you cannot go to the operating room with it in. I cannot put you to sleep with a foreign body in your mouth."

Foreign body! Audrey felt the blood leave her head. Gongs could not have sounded louder in her ears. Then a final cold ticking.

"For how long . . . ?"

"Until you are fully awake. Certainly till evening."

"But you don't understand . . ." she began. Her voice trailed off. The doctor waited, turned his head, looked at her from the corner of an eye.

"Yes?"

"It is . . . My husband does not know that I have a denture. He has been unaware of it for fifteen years. I would not want him to see me without it. Please," she said very quietly. "It is important to me." She waited for the walls to burst.

"Pride," said the man. "No room for it here. Like modesty. Suppose we had to get at your trachea, your windpipe, in a hurry, and then we had to waste time fishing those teeth out. Suppose they came loose in the middle of the operation. There are a hundred supposes." He started to go.

"It isn't pride," she managed.

"What, then?"

"It's dignity." Perhaps it had been pride at the very beginning, but it had grown. And something else: Audrey understood that the connubial apparatus of a man is more delicate than a woman's. She saw no need to put it to the test.

"Come now. Mrs. Blakeslee, is it?" He consulted the name on the chart to make sure. Audrey struggled to fend off his voice. "You are making too much of it."

All right, then, she would calculate, be a cat.

"Don't you . . ." she began. "Don't you have a little something hidden away that you wouldn't want anyone to know about?" She smiled, laying it on in almost visible slabs. The doctor was taken off guard.

"No, actually not." But he had hesitated for the fraction of a second, and so she knew.

"How boring," she said, smiling, giving it to him right in his face. "And, of course, I don't for a minute believe you." This doctor could not know it, but Audrey was fighting for her life. But now she saw that he had retreated a vast safe distance behind his lips.

"In any case, you may not keep them in. And that's that." He stood abruptly and walked to the door.

"Have a good night," he called over his shoulder.

After he had left, Audrey felt her heart go small in her chest. Again there was the clink of coins being stirred in a pocket. With a sudden resolve, she decided that there was no longer any need for tact. The situation didn't call for tact. It called for defiance. I'll sign myself out of the hospital, she thought. Against medical advice, as they say. That cyst on her ovary, it might well be benign. They don't know. Leaving it in would be just one more risk. A risk infinitely smaller than having Leonard see her without her denture. Her mouth caved in, wrinkled like a drawstring pouch. She tried to imagine herself saying to Leonard afterward: "All right, then. You have seen what you have seen. Now accept it. Or not." But she could not. That way lay death. Hers or that of something far more delicate and valuable. No, she thought. No. Never again would she cultivate a belief in inevitability.

Audrey reached for the telephone, dialed.

"Leonard, don't come to the hospital at all tomorrow."

"But why?" He was startled. "Of course I'm coming to see you."

"That's just the point, Leonard, please . . ." She heard her voice flapping about her, out of control. "Please." She was imploring him.

"Don't come. Promise me."

"I'm sorry, Audrey. I'm just not going to agree to that. So forget it." His tone was severe, as with a child.

"I don't want you to see me like that."

"Like what?" He smiled with his voice. "I have seen it all before, you know." Oh, but you haven't, she thought. You shouldn't.

"What is it, Audrey? You sound distraught. Shall I come right over? I'll make them let me in."

"I just wanted to spare you," she said harshly. "There are times when people need to be alone."

"No," said Leonard. "I'll be there."

Violet managed the gift shop in the lobby of the hospital. She was two years older than Audrey—a big woman, divorced once, widowed once. Violet did not use makeup. I have nothing to hide, she said. Still, she dyed her hair. For business reasons. When you have to meet the public, gray hair automatically dismisses you. Fifteen years before, they had been closer, when Violet had brought her home from the dentist's office and Audrey had sworn her to a lifetime of silence. But somewhere between then and now Vi had become the kind of woman who sat herself down with ceremony in a deep chair to receive the secrets of others. She would be coming up to the room after she closed the gift shop. Audrey would ask her for a ride home. She would deal with Leonard later.

"I'll do no such thing," said Violet. "Do you mean to lie there and tell me that Leonard still doesn't know about your false teeth?" Vi made a point of never saying "denture." "False teeth" had a balder sound and they had drifted too far apart for softness. The venules on Vi's cheeks dilated with indignant blood. Audrey reached for the light switch, flicked it off. It was something to do.

"May I turn off the light?" she asked then. In the dark she could see the glossy mound of her sister's hair.

"Listen, Audrey, this has become a sick obsession with you." Her vehemence was reiterated by flashes of gold at neck and earlobes.

"There are madder things," said Audrey. And she lamented the weakness that made her let down her guard before this stranger who was her sister.

"Besides, it's a lie. People shouldn't lie, whatever."

"Oh, lies," said Audrey. "That's where you're wrong. People don't lie enough. When people tell the whole truth, that's when things fall apart. Most relationships are like some plants, I think. They need to be kept partly in the shade or they wither." A nurse came in and turned on the light. In the sudden glare Violet leaped up at her.

"Now, Audrey, don't be stupid," she said, standing to leave. "Behave yourself." Violet's teeth would never fall out, Audrey thought. They chew words, worry them; the way they buckle up her mouth.

Almost at once there was a hesitant knock at the door. Oh, God. Now who?

"My name is Dr. Bhimjee. I am the intern on this ward." An Indian or Pakistani, she thought. And lame. He limped toward the bed using his head and one arm in the act of locomotion.

88

"Mrs. Blakeslee, I see that our names both end with two *e*'s." His face was dark, she suspected, more from fatigue than from racial coloring. More than anything else he resembled an ungainly parcel, something bulgy and ill-wrapped. His hair was almost too thick, too black, but relieved by a single swatch of white near the crown. He is not young, Audrey decided. What has he endured and with how much patience? All at once, a fence came down. Who, after all, is to say where, in whom, one places trust?

"I have false teeth," she said, firing the words into his hair. She was shocked at the ease with which the forbidden words had come. The intern gazed down at her.

"Many people do," he said. The slate-colored skin set off the perfection of his own very white teeth. He is beautiful, she thought. And she threw herself further upon his mercy.

"I have had them for fifteen years. My husband has never seen me without them. He doesn't know that I have them. The anesthetist was here. He says I must leave them here in the room tomorrow. My husband will be waiting for me to come back from the recovery room. He will see me. I can't do that. Please, please." The last words rose like echoes. For a long moment they looked at each other, during which something, a covenant perhaps, Audrey did not know, was exchanged. Audrey lashed her gaze to his long gracile fingers. Then, all at once, deep called unto deep. A rush of profound affection came over her. It was nothing like her feeling for Leonard, but for all she knew, it might have been love.

"Do not worry." The *r*'s rolled very slightly. "In the morning, put them in the nightstand. There is a container. I will take them with me to the operation. I am assigned to your case, so I will be there too. Before you leave the recovery room, I will put them back into your mouth. Do not worry."

Later, when she awoke in the recovery room, the pain of her incision was the second thing that Audrey felt. The first was the denture which she explored with her tongue. Only then came the pain which, so help her, she did not mind. In spite of it, she curled up like a cat in a basket. Once, when she opened her eyes, she saw, or thought she saw, a dark face above her, a white swatch in a tumble of black hair, like a plume of smoke clinging to the chimney of a snug cottage.

"Don't worry," he was saying softly. "Your teeth are in. Take a deep breath. Again." He listened with his stethoscope. "You will be awake soon." He checked her pulse, and was gone. For a long time his voice lingered, lapsing, returning, drifting into darkness. And then there was Leonard, holding her hand, leaning over the bed to kiss her. "The doctor says it was benign." Audrey smiled up at him within the limits of morphine.

During the days that followed, Audrey found herself thinking about Dr. Bhimjee as much as she did about Leonard. There was a peacefulness about him. Not resignation so much as acceptance. No, definitely not resignation. Resignation suggests defeat. Acceptance, rather. Where had he found it? Wrested it, she supposed, barehanded from a tangle of thorns. He had no need to deceive. It had not been given to him to deceive. She saw him differently now from the way she had that first desperate night. What she had thought was fatigue became the sum total of all the suffering he had experienced. It had worn his face down to the bone. The sockets of his eyes were dark cabins of it. Audrey would have liked to take the bony parcel in her arms, to breathe in his dreams.

And soon it was the hour of Audrey's discharge from the hospital. The intern had come to say good-bye.

"My wife tells me that you have been very kind to her,"

said Leonard. Audrey could not take her gaze from the two men.

"Not at all."

"I want you to know that I will always remember your" —she saw that Leonard was struggling—"your courtesy."

"Please, it was nothing."

"Nevertheless," said Leonard. "Nevertheless," he repeated, "I want you to have this." He held out a small reddish stone.

"What is that?"

"Just a stone that has been dyed red by the Asmat people of New Guinea. See? It has a monkey carved on one side, a parrot on the other. A shaman gave it to me. He's a sort of doctor too. It wards off melancholy, brings good luck. Please, take it." The doctor hesitated.

"I want you to have it," said Leonard. There was in his voice something vivid, mighty. Maybe it was the sun probing between the slats of the venetian blinds, but from her wheelchair it seemed to Audrey that, at the exact moment when the red stone left the white hand of one and entered the dark hand of the other, something flared up that looked for all the world like fire.

"The Black Swan" Revisited

In Homage to Thomas Mann

PREFACE

The impulse to rewrite "The Black Swan" came less from
the desire to pay homage to Thomas Mann, although that
is surely what I shall always wish to do, than from a scene
momentarily witnessed at the hospital where I work. I was
on evening rounds and I passed the open door of a room
occupied by someone who was not my own patient. Glancing in without breaking stride, I saw a very old and ema-
ciated woman lying propped on pillows. She could have
weighed no more than seventy pounds. Every bone threatened to burst through parchment. Her hands were spiders
at the end of sticks. No matter, she was totally engaged in
working a long gold pendant earring through her earlobe.
Her head was inclined toward shaking fingers; a look of
fierce concentration pleated her face as she probed for the
hole. This I saw, and nothing more. But it constituted a
moment of clarity in which her act of adornment took on
incalculable significance. Once again, a hospital bed had
been transformed into a draperied couch by the person
lying in it. In that moment the old woman had taken on

for me the persona of Rosalie von Tummler, and I knew that I would begin to tell her story again that very night.

In that period of deception between the two great wars, in the city of Düsseldorf-on-the-Rhine, on an almost fashionable street called Magenstrasse, there lived a widow, Rosalie von Tummler, and her two children. From the beginning, Edward, a pale spidery boy of seventeen, had been slated by his father for a military career. Come October he was to leave for the Academy. The elder, Anna, a spinster of twenty-eight, had been born with a clubfoot which had resisted a series of attempts at surgical correction. From childhood on she had studied art and only lately had developed a small reputation in the city for her paintings. Herr von Tummler, may God rest his soul, had died ten years before in an accident the details of which to this day remained fuzzy in his widow's mind. It had to do, Rosalie understood vaguely, with another woman. But it had never occurred to her to be resentful. That was a man's nature, and Rosalie was prepared to accept nature in all of its numberless aspects. Rosalie attributed her sensitivity to the natural world to having been born in April when every living thing on the planet was beginning what she called its "grand investigation." Often, on her birdwatching or rock-collecting treks, she could almost hear the slow rising of the sap in the trees or the infinitesimally small noise of plant cells dividing and multiplying. When she told this to the children, Edward would circle one of his ears with a finger and Anna would smile.

It was this same acceptance of nature's ways that had enabled Rosalie to go through her change of life some five years before with equanimity. For her, none of the irritability, headaches, hot flashes and melancholy of other women. Sensibly, Rosalie rejected these symptoms and, in the end, declared herself relieved to have it all over with.

No event in nature, she said to Anna, is without its purpose.

As luck would have it, Herr von Tummler had left a moderate inheritance, and so the three were able to live, if not in luxury, in a state very far from deprivation. Within those limits Rosalie had seen to it that the household was decorous and calm, and that the talents of each of her children were developed as far as possible. She herself had taken courses in botany and zoology at the university, even going so far as to dissect a fetal pig. Had she been a man, she told Anna, she would have been a scientist. As it was, she studied and collected things. Frau von Tummler was one of those small women who, in middle age, take on a certain physical solidity. Still, she had what might be called an elderly beauty. For instance, she had not entirely lost her figure, the bosom and hips being accentuated by the narrower waist about which she always wore a belt, or a sash with an elusive pattern. The open wide smile was still there, and her heavy braids, while dusted with gray, were full. Twisted and secured about her head they shone in the sunlight. In fact, the more one gazed at Rosalie von Tummler, the nearer one came to the image of a pretty young woman of years ago. Now and then, Anna would be coaxed into accompanying her mother on one of her specimen-gathering walks in the countryside. From the distance, seeing the petite mother's graceful stride, taking one step to every limping one and a half of the taller, thinner, prematurely dessicated Anna, one would have guessed their roles reversed. Anna's clubfoot had made intimates of them, each confiding in the other without embarrassment.

With just the same equanimity as Rosalie had accepted the biological news of her menopause, so had Anna one day set down her easel for a moment, gazed at some distant horizon, then accepted her spinsterhood. Anna's paintings were in the abstract mode. To Rosalie, the naturalist, the canvases held nothing recognizable. She simply did not understand them. Try as she might to conjure a leaf or a bird in flight from a shapeless swirl of the brush, she could not.

"How do you do it?" she asked Anna.

"First, I make a mark with the brush. This leads me to the second stroke. These two, their relationship to each other, induce the third, and so on."

"How do you know when it is done?"

"When there is no more room on the canvas," Anna laughed.

The week prior to Anna's twenty-ninth birthday, Rosalie saw on the back page of the newspaper a small discreet advertisement for private English lessons to be given at the homes of the pupils. The name of the teacher was Ken Keaton. English, thought Rosalie. No, American. The Ken gives it away. Immediately, she decided to present these lessons to Anna for her birthday, and arranged an interview by mail. A young American in his middle twenties arrived. Pleased with his informal manner and his Irish good looks, Rosalie at once pronounced him suitable. It was decided that he would come every Tuesday and Thursday at four o'clock. The lessons would take place in the parlor to which large French doors would give privacy and where teacher and pupil might work uninterrupted by the noise of the household. Anna declared herself delighted with her present, and so it happened that Ken Keaton entered the placid rhythm of the house on Magenstrasse. Twice each week at precisely five minutes to four in the afternoon, Rosalie would answer the knocking at the door and lead the young man to the oval mahogany table in the bay window of the parlor. She would pull the draperies across the window and leave. Moments later there would be the heavy drag of Anna's footstep on the stairs. In this way, weeks went by. Now and then, Rosalie would tiptoe to the closed door, press her ear against it, and when she heard Anna responding to the teacher's question in English, she would shiver with a mother's satisfaction.

It must be said that to a woman of Rosalie's romantic nature the thought that an affection might grow between her daughter and the young man had more than once entered her mind. She had once or twice felt wistful about the possibility. But just as quickly she would dismiss the notion. Not likely, she would think. Not for Anna. But still . . .

"He's a nice young man, isn't he?" she said to Anna.

"Quite nice, yes."

"Really, what do you think of him?"

"Really, Mother, I don't think of him much." Rosalie was not ungrateful for the terminal placement of that "much."

Once, the lesson having gone on for some minutes past the hour, Rosalie knocked on the door, excused herself, and suggested to Ken that he stay for dinner. He accepted at once. The evening had proved pleasant and sociable. It was the first of many dinners Ken Keaton was to take at the von Tummlers'. At times it seemed to Anna that he would purposely prolong the lesson to position himself for an invitation. Each time, when asked, he would accept without hesitation. As often as not, immediately after coffee, Anna would excuse herself and clomp upstairs to her studio, leaving the two others to linger at the table. Rosalie would pour Ken a brandy and herself a glass of port. Now and then Rosalie was acutely conscious that Anna could hear them laughing from upstairs. At such times, she would feel a twinge of guilt.

One day, Rosalie sat at the small table where the lessons took place. She did not hear him enter the room. Only when he had come to stand in her line of vision, blocking out her view of the sky and the garden outside, did she notice. At first, she tried to peer around him in annoyance, then felt her focus shortening from the world beyond the window to the world this side of it, which at that moment was filled to the exclusion of all else with the body of Ken Keaton.

Rosalie could not have said just when it happened that she fell in love with him, what specific sight or sound had caused desire, long outgrown, to bounce back to its feet. Had it been that hot August day when he arrived in shorts and sleeveless shirt? Then, at the sight of the tufts of light brown hair at his armpits, each strand bearing a droplet of perspiration, she had smelled his sweat and felt herself redden.

"What is that?" she bent over him, studying the bunched violet scar on his thigh. It was star-shaped, the pitted center being of the deepest hue, and paling out along the points, one of which disappeared beneath the cloth of his shorts. Here and there a ridge caught the light and shone tightly.

"I was wounded," said Ken simply. He made no move to cover it. Instead, with an unselfconsciousness that Rosalie had come to think of as peculiarly American, he pulled up his shorts to show her more.

"It goes even higher," he said.

"Is it painful still?"

"No. Only now and then when I sweat, it itches as though something, a bug, were crawling on it, something that I cannot scratch."

That night Rosalie could not sleep. In the turmoil of her bed she closed her eyes and saw the scar again and again, the way it wandered up beneath his shorts to end . . . where? All at once, she sat upright, her heart pounding. What is the matter with me? she thought. What is happening to me? And clapped one hand over her mouth because what she wanted to do more than anything was to run her tongue over that scar.

Or had it been the day when, unobserved, she had watched them through the barely opened door to the parlor? Anna and Ken were speaking softly. She could not hear them. So profoundly were they absorbed, so still, that they seemed to Rosalie to be figures woven into a tapestry. Anna's face appeared dark, smudged in half light; Ken's, illuminated by the lamp, was a forbidden spectacle—something like a transfiguration. When, suddenly, he caught sight of her and smiled, she had to lean against the door. In any case, from that moment, Rosalie felt a circle had been drawn about her out of which she could not step. Intemperate! she thought. That was the word for it. You would think that a lifetime of propriety would offer some immunity against a rashness that could end only in humiliation. Again and again she tried to think of her husband, dead these many years. But all she could remember of him was the monocle he wore and which every little while he would disimpact from his eyesocket and wipe. And the gold incisor tooth which in the early days of her marriage had given her that extra feeling of opulence when he kissed her. Who, she asked herself, what, was this Ken Keaton who seemed to live from day to day without much vivacity or wit? He was nothing. Yet there was something like distinction or heroism about him. Remembering his face, Rosalie decided that it was the genius of beauty.

Had she been offered a choice—whether to stay as she had been, in a state of harmony, enjoying nature, her children, her garden—or to fall in love, she would have rejected the abstraction of Ken Keaton. But that was not given her. Love, she discovered, cannot be elected or declined. Like illness, it comes, and that is that. Rosalie felt there was something violent and graceless about her suffering. Surely it would give her away. Now and then, without warning, saliva would gather in her mouth; once it had made her choke. Or sweat would spring to her upper lip and nose. At such times, she would weep for the hopelessness of it. The gnawing pain of it. The beauty.

She could not keep her gaze from him. Once, feeling perhaps the hot point of it between his shoulder blades, he turned so suddenly that she had been caught off guard and had burst into awkward tears that to the young man were inexplicable.

"What is it?" he asked. "Is something the matter?"

"Nothing. It is nothing. A sudden female emotion. It is not unheard of at my age. Pay it no mind." He had smiled then, in relief. My God! She must be more careful.

Another time, he had come upon her unexpectedly while she was cutting roses in the garden. Beautiful, he had said. The roses leaped in her hand. A drop of blood bloomed at her fingertip. Oh, she had said. Look! And she had held it up for him to see. At once he turned his face aside.

"Ugh! Blood," he said. "I hate the sight of it."

How lucky other women are, she thought, keeping on with their moderately turning lives while she felt herself wasting from a grotesque desire. In the heightened isolation of love, she would think of these others, the women of her neighborhood, as sheep mindlessly grazing. One day toward the beginning of April, returning from the market, Rosalie was hailed by her friend Lisa who also had been widowed but was now unhappily remarried.

"You seem, Rosalie, to have come through the winter with ever greater liveliness than before. There is such a color in your cheeks. Is it rouge? And you have become slender! Look, it's true." And she encircled Rosalie's waist with her arm. "If I did not know you better, I would say that you have taken a lover." The woman laughed. Rosalie was certain that the pounding of her heart and the fluttering of the lace collar of her dress was noticed. She held one hand to the collar, but the woman had not seen.

"It is easier," Lisa went on, "for a woman alone to find happiness. Domesticity, and all that goes with it—boredom, frustrated passion—it ages one so."

"Lisa . . ." said Rosalie. But she could speak no more than the woman's name.

As for sleep, it was a place she could not enter. She would urge herself toward it, but a gate was barred. She was like an animal trying to crawl back into its lair, only to find the burrow blocked by heavy stones. But it was at the dinner table that Rosalie fully engaged her martyrdom. A dozen times during a meal she spied on his face, eating him with her eyes. He filled her so that she could eat nothing else.

"You have eaten nothing," Anna once said. Instead of speaking, Rosalie raised her wineglass to her lips and kept watch for the moist tip of his tongue when he opened his mouth to eat. What had she fed upon, what had nourished her, before this? For the life of her, she could not remember.

As Rosalie stood to refill his glass, pouring the wine as though it were a sacrament, she caught sight of herself in the tarnished mirror on the wall. The face she saw was a face in pain and which gave pain. The line, like a deep fault that, year after year, rose farther from the bridge of her nose to bisect her forehead, there was no smoothing it out. All at once a single violent tremor shook her hand so that the stream of red wine wobbled over the dark wood of the table. She felt the quick glance of the other two.

"Never mind," said Anna, mopping with her napkin. But Rosalie stared at the scattered red puddles that remained. It shocked her to think just how far she had departed from life before the arrival of Ken. When she looked back upon her years of serene widowhood, she felt only that they held a kind of obsolete charm to which she could no longer relate. The whole idea of her former life was what she had relinquished. She would not return to it again. Now she seemed to be outlined by a frame, waiting for something to happen.

Just so did the autumn pass unnoticed by the suffering woman. It was Christmas Eve when Rosalie told Anna. Mother and daughter had been trimming the tree.

"Anna," she said. "Your mother is a foolish old woman."

"What now?" laughed Anna.

"I have fallen in love. With Ken," she said simply.

Anna stood motionless and turned to study her mother's face, reading there what she had never seen before: humiliation and naked pleasure.

"But that is ridiculous. He is younger than I am."

"Yes. That is what is so terrible and unnatural. Nevertheless, it is true. I cannot deceive myself." Suddenly, the older woman sank to her knees, her body shaking with sobs.

"What is it that you feel?" said Anna gently. "Try to say exactly." Rosalie shrugged and shook her head. She could not put the symptoms of love into words any more than a woman, immediately after childbirth, can describe the pain of it. Only, she knew, that it must find release or she would die of it. There were times when her body was uninhabitable for another instant. There was no room for her in it. Something else was crowding her out.

"Why don't you try writing it down?" said Anna. "Just putting it into words on a page will make it recede. In any case, you might feel better. I read somewhere that there is an ancient magic in writing a sorrow down, then burning the paper upon which it is written. It makes the affliction go away. Perhaps it will work for a hopeless desire as well." When Anna left the room, Rosalie sat at the writing table and did indeed try to write it all down. Yes, she would burn the paper, and when she saw the thing writhe in the flames, she would be rid of it. But all that appeared on the papers were the words *Ken* and *Love*. In the end she could not bring herself to throw the piece of paper into the fire. It would be an unnatural act, she decided.

Even in Anna's absence, she fought with herself. It is not love, she would argue. It is lust. An obsession with his body. After all, she knew nothing about his mind, which was a territory she was little moved to explore. But no, said Rosalie aloud in the privacy of her room. No. It is love. To call it anything else—infatuation, obsession—would be an act of cowardice. And a lie. I love him.

"But it is dangerous," said Anna. "There is the possibility of ridicule. You must admit that there is something a bit . . . well . . . laughable about it."

"I suppose there is. Yes, laughable. But Sarah laughed at the idea of getting a child with Abraham at the age of ninety-nine."

"Can't you just like him for what he represents? Youth, good health, an intact body, potential?" Anna was running out of patience with her mother. "Can't you just adore him spiritually? It would be so much more sensible."

"Does he know?" asked Anna. Rosalie shook her head. But he must know, she thought. On some level, he must be aware. The little half smiles he gave her. Was he young and callow enough to be flattered? Pleased to have made a conquest? Any conquest? Yes! That was it exactly. But Rosalie did not care. I will have him on any terms, she thought miserably.

That night in her room Rosalie studied herself in the mirror. Why, Lisa was right, she thought. Despite everything, I must say I look well. I have not grown into an old woman. She stepped nearer to the glass, peering for evidence. It was true. Her hair was quite lively in the lamplight; it had certainly grown no grayer. And she had lost just enough weight to rid her of that bit of thickening around the middle. I am slender, she said aloud. As the days went by, Rosalie's preoccupation with her appearance grew. Each night, she would stand before the mirror in her room, examining. It seemed to her that her eyes were once again as bright as a girl's. The skin of her arms and neck was pale, pale as ivory. And smooth. She had always been proud of her complexion. But this! Is this what love does to a woman? she thought. Try as she might to brush aside the notion, she could not entirely rid herself of the idea that she looked younger than she had in years. Certainly, she felt younger. Even her voice had taken on a clear girlishness. One night, in fact, she dreamed that she had been given the body of a young girl.

Six months to the day after Ken's first visit to the house on the Magenstrasse, Rosalie von Tummler lay in her bed and did battle. It was past midnight and through the drawn curtain a shifty moon teased. Black leaves waggled at the windowsill. Another night of it, she thought. Slowly, all but imperceptibly, she felt the first cramp building low in her abdomen. It grew big, the way thunder grows big from the smallest beginning, and rolled as thunder rolls before ebbing away. In a moment, another, and another. It has reached the point of pain, thought Rosalie, and turned on her side, drawing her knees up, pressing them into her belly, squeezing the pain from her body. How much further was there to go? Even her breasts felt the longing; they were tender, engorged, the nipples registering discomfort beneath the sheets. The curled position gave her relief and presently she fell asleep. It was still dark when she awoke. Rosalie pushed herself upward to sit on the edge of the bed, to stand and leave that bed which had just given her so little rest and so much suffering. As she stood, Rosalie felt a warmth moving on her inner thigh, then something slide down her leg. She put her hand there to feel a moisture. Even before she saw the dark stain on her fingers, she knew that it was blood. It is happening, she marveled. I am menstruating! Once again, a woman, after so many years. It is the miracle of love. Love, she thought, is making me young again to be worthy of him. Of course! How is it that I had not recognized it before this? The tenderness and sensitivity of my breasts, the cramps. A wave of triumph swept her body.

How differently men and women think about bleeding. For Rosalie it bore the promise of love and youth. Whereas Ken . . . Had he not told her that day in the garden when she pricked herself, had he not told her that he could not stand the sight of blood? It is the men who are frail. They perceive the shedding of so much as a single drop of their blood as a reminder that they will one day sicken and die. In three days, the bleeding had stopped. Rosalie noted the dwindling of the flow, then the cessation, almost with reluctance. When, the next month, she experienced the premonitory signs, she was overjoyed and gave herself up to the anticipation of the flow. She was not disappointed; there was again pain and bleeding. Again! she thought. She could not wait to tell Anna.

"Anna! Anna!" she called. But Anna had gone for a walk. Rosalie waited impatiently for her daughter to return. She died to tell her the news. At last she saw from the upstairs window the younger woman limping up the walk, and she rapped a signal on the pane with her thimble. Even then, she thought that, minus her limp, Anna would be unnoticeable.

"But, Mama, you are imagining it." Anna looked genuinely frightened as though she had heard evidence of her mother's insanity.

"Miracles!" said Anna, unable to keep the contempt out of her tone. "It is so unlike you, Mama. All your life you have preferred facts and virtues. Now, suddenly you depend upon miracles. Which is the more reliable, I ask you?" When her mother made no reply, Anna felt the anger mounting within her.

"How could you have let this happen?"

"That is easy for you to say," said Rosalie. "Love is a hardship which you have been spared."

Anna looked down at her mother, saw the violet swatch that had lately appeared beneath each of her eyes.

"If this be love, I'll have none of it."

Anna knew that her mother would never renounce him. She had never learned the art of renunciation. As I have, she thought. As I have had to.

"Then there is only one thing to do, as I see it," she said. "You must tell him."

"And if he refuses? Makes fun of me?"

"You must prepare yourself for that."

"I should not live long after that," said Rosalie quietly. "I should not want to."

Anna's eyes filled with tears. "But that is a terrible thing to say. Don't I mean anything to you? Doesn't Edward? Mama, if he refuses you, the sky will still be blue, the grass green. There will be still all of your beloved nature. Aren't these reasons for going on? And besides," she added, "there is always the possibility . . ."

"We must choose a time and a place then."

"Not in this house," said Anna quickly. "There is Edward, after all."

"Where then?"

"An outing. The four of us. We'll pack a picnic lunch and take the boat up the Rhine to the park. The one with the old castle and the bird pond."

"When?"

"The sooner the better. This Sunday. At least we shall know."

Standing on the deck of the boat, Rosalie stared into the wake and could not tell in which direction the river was flowing. It was as though she were seeing it for the first time, seeing it as it really was. It seemed to her that she was standing in the teeth of a wind although the air was calm save for the small breeze of their passage. For weeks she had wondered how he would respond to her declaration. Now, here, on the boat she permitted herself a moment of confidence. After all, it was spring. The banks were every shade of green. There was the silent tide of sap, the speckled eggs that she knew lay hidden in the bushes. One day soon, boughs would be parted; a tiny new bird would be disgorged from straining shrubbery. No summer, however splendid, could fulfill the prophecy of such a spring. Had not nature given her back her youth to be worthy of his love? Only two days before, she had finished with her monthly flow. Again! And with each flux she felt age flowing away from her. To what blessed state was she returning? How far into youth would the miracle take her? A wave of giddiness overtook her so that she had to cling to the railing of the boat. If she had let herself go at that moment, she could have fainted.

It had been arranged between mother and daughter that Anna and Edward would go off to explore the gardens while Rosalie and Ken would visit the old castle ruin. An hour later, they were to meet at the pond. It would have been settled by then. One way or the other. Rosalie watched her children walking away from her. Go! Go! she thought in a burst of impatience. Then she turned to Ken, slipped her arm through his and drew him toward the ancient pile of stone that had been a castle and that lay half tumbled down the slope of a long lawn. An empty moat surrounded the ruin. They crossed the bridge and walked around to the far side where an expectant archway led to a flight of descending stone steps, each one spotted with a rash of gray lichen. At the bottom of the stairs was a stone door to what must have been a cellar. Ken tried the door but it was locked and bolted. The steps were moist and slimy, covered with rotting leaves. The smell of mold and earth filled the well. At the bottom, they were quite hidden from view. Rosalie had untied the ends of her veil and they hung limply over her shoulders, like braids of pale girlish hair. All at once she heard herself calling out his name, "Ken! Ken!" in a voice so clear and young it startled her. Minutes later she was clinging to him unable to control the sobbing breaths that chased the confession from her mouth. At last, he lifted her chin and bent to kiss her.

"When?" he asked. "Where?"

Rosalie grew suddenly calm as though a storm had passed. Only the odor of decaying leaves gave her a feeling of queasiness.

"Tomorrow. Three o'clock. The café across the square from the library. There are rooms upstairs." Leaning into his embrace, Rosalie felt the stones of the old wall stir gently. She listened and heard the honey-colored sap flowing in the trees nearby, saw the beads of it press themselves between the ridges of bark. It was not his kiss but the whole weight of the eternal afternoon that pressed the breath from her parted lips. She felt that she needed twice as much oxygen as anyone else, and she thanked God for the pressure of Ken's hand at her waist, stilling her, calling her back from a state beyond control.

"A terrible stench," said Ken, "these rotting leaves. Let's go back now." At the top of the steps a sudden shaft of sunlight struck, making her stagger. Ken disengaged his arm from hers and bent to scrape away the damp leaves that had become stuck to the soles of his shoes. Then once again, arm in arm, they walked toward the pond.

From the distance she saw them, up to their wings in the water, motionless. Three pairs of white swans. And a single black.

". . . two, three, four, five, six, seven," she counted. "That's something! And all so lovely." She was wild with excitement. "But the black. He is another matter entirely. See how he shovels the water with that red bill of his. And he is alone. He has no mate. I do like him the best."

Ken fished in his pocket. "The bread," he said. "I almost forgot that we brought it to feed them." At the familiar gesture, the black swan swam toward them. All at once, Rosalie snatched the bread from Ken's hand, still warm from the heat of his body and stuffed it into her mouth. Furious at having been cheated, the black swan raised its wings as though for flight, then thrust toward her, hissing through its blood-red bill. So close did the great bird come to the bank that the shadow of its lifted wings touched Rosalie's feet. She took a quick step backward and threw the rest of the bread to the angry swan. Then Rosalie laughed, throwing the laughter from her throat like lumps of gristle. It was less a human sound than an issuance more akin to the hissing of the swan. Shocked, Ken turned to stare at her, to see from what galled place it had come forth. But Rosalie took no notice.

Once again aboard the riverboat, Rosalie stood alone upon the deck. The others had retreated from the evening chill to the ward room where tea was being served. Far from refreshing her spirit, Rosalie found the river depressing. Sluggish, this Rhine, she thought. Almost stagnant. Breeding flies as though it were a dead animal. Furthermore, she felt unwell. Febrile. When she looked from side to side, her eyeballs ached. The touch of the breeze on her skin was unbearable. She was panting as though the air found passage through her veil difficult. Her head was like a torch in the wind. She was being consumed. Still, gripping the iron railing, she yawned with suppressed desire. Her womb had turned molten with it.

That night Rosalie fell into a deep sleep from which she was coaxed hours later by the rhythmic pounding of driven rain upon the roof. In her half-awakened state she imagined hooves galloping across the slate. All at once, she became aware of a familiar sensation of warmth and moisture between her thighs. A tickling. A cramp rolled across her belly. But it is too soon, she thought. It is not my time. She threw back the covers, raised her head to see. And saw the great dark glistening clot that covered her abdomen and thighs, the puddling in the sheets.

"Anna!" she screamed. "Anna!" And fainted back upon the pillow.

Anna waited in the hospital solarium for the doctor to complete his examination. At last he appeared.

"Cancer," he said. "The neck of the womb. It is beyond surgery, I'm afraid. We must resort to radium to control the bleeding. She is receiving blood transfusions now." He paused. "It is not good." He spoke more softly. "We are in trouble here."

Rosalie awoke to find the doctor standing at the bedside.

". . . radium therapy," she heard him say.

"Shall I be cured then?"

"That? . . . No. It is meant to stop the bleeding, to give time." His gaze was solemn, not unkind. He was used to this, she saw. Perhaps as a younger man, he had practiced the expression.

"And the pain?"

"Morphine," he said. Rosalie shook her head.

"I think not," she said at last.

"You will not undergo the radium treatments?" The

doctor's voice had a note of incredulity. "But surely you do not wish to bleed to death?"

Her voice was calm and final. "There are symptoms too merciful to be placed in the hands of a doctor."

"Be reasonable, Frau von Tummler. It is unnatural to reject the assistance of medical science. Some would call it suicide."

"Some," said Rosalie, "would be wrong." With distaste she submitted to the pressure of his fingers at her pulse. For a minute he counted in silence.

"But what, then, is the point of my attending you?"

"None, I think." She closed her eyes and waited for him to withdraw.

At the door, he turned, and Rosalie imagined she heard him click his heels faintly.

"Frau von Tummler," he said, acknowledging his dismissal.

In the six weeks since the outing in the park, Rosalie had shed what seemed half of her body. A collapsed pouch, she thought, looking down at what remained in the bed. She felt empty, yet strangely heavy, as though her weight had doubled, rather than halved. Her arm, when she tried to lift it from the sheet, was as tired as if it had been holding up a candle for her to see her way down an interminable corridor.

"No," she thought. "I shall not be so foolish as to escape a benevolent and easy death. The doctor is wrong. It is very far from suicide. That other: the radium, the morphine, that is how the doctors swindle human beings." Still, she knew, there would be Anna to deal with.

To Anna the woman on the bed had the look of a young girl, as though the illness, with its fever and wasting, had returned her to a state of . . . well . . . girlishness. She could think of no other word. She gazed down at the long thick braids hanging at either side of her mother's face, by their very immensity accentuating the tiny fragile chin. Now, thought Anna sadly, you have your wish.

"The doctor says that the radium is essential," said Anna.

"Does he?"

"The doctor says you have no alternative."

"Don't I? Listen, Anna, my darling. It is cowardice that causes people to wait to die by the doctor's hand. I am bestowing it upon myself. Bleeding to death is painless. It is a death reserved for the righteous. How much worse had I outlived him, if he had been killed in an accident, or he had rejected me, then I should have died of shame. No, this is best. Only, those nearby . . . you, Anna . . . ought not to soil yourselves with it. That is what would not be natural. Besides, how lucky I am. That death came to me in the guise of love. To how many is that given?" She leaned forward and looked deep into Anna's eyes. "You must know that I want him now as much as ever."

When Anna had left the room, Rosalie sank back upon the pillows. The effort she had made for Anna had drained her of strength. It was true, her longing had lost none of its virulence. Again and again her thoughts returned to that day in the park. Never, never had there been so sweet a day, when, giddy to the point of fainting, she had buried her face in his shoulder and clung to him as much, if the truth be known, to keep herself from falling as to hold him in her desperate grasp. And she had babbled so. Her very words had all but carried her away. "You do not think me too old, then?" She could not speak, and yet she was speaking. Be still, he had said. Not so loud. The others will hear. And he had pressed her to him, hushing. Sssh, he had said. Ssssh, until she had felt no further need for words. And when the laugh rose from low in his chest, she had at first mistrusted. Was it the mockery she had dreaded? But when she saw him radiant and smiling, she knew that he had accepted her.

Ken had not visited her at the hospital. At first, she had hoped against all reason that he would, that he would come and take her up in his arms and stroke her back to health. But she knew that he would not come, and she was satisfied with that, forgave him. Why should he come? she thought. He has the innocence of the well. Such innocence must be preserved for as long as possible. There would be plenty of time for death. There always is. And just as she had decided that, there was the nurse telling her that a young man was waiting in the lobby to see her and should she show him up? Yes! Yes! she said in a voice full of longing. The nurse helped her into her bed jacket. Rosalie brushed back her hair with three strokes of a transparent hand. So he has come, she thought. And waited for the nurse to return with Ken. Oh, God, the dark seam of her lips, her yellow skin?

My earrings, she thought. I must wear them. She reached for the drawer of her nightstand. The effort, or was it the pain she kept hidden beneath the sheets, made her dizzy. At last, fumbling, she had them. Long pendants of gold that hung almost to her shoulders. Her husband had given them to her before Edward was born. She had always thought them a bit indiscreet for a married woman and had not worn them in years. All at once, it seemed the most urgent thing for her to wear them when he entered her room. She must hurry. He would be there within minutes. Rosalie raised one earring to her neck groping shakily for the lobe of her ear. Supporting the working arm with the opposite hand, she grimaced with the effort. At last, she found the little hole and passed the wire through. Now the other. But try as she might, holding her head to the side, pulling her earlobe down to searching exhausted fingers, she could do no more than poke the skin with the cold metal. Again and again she jabbed blindly for the hole, all of her strength and will engaged in this act of adornment. At last, she sank back helplessly and gave it up. Her eyes closed on tears of disappointment. She had wanted so much to be wearing them. So that at first she did not see him standing in the doorway. When she opened her eyes and saw, saw not only Ken, but what had settled there on his face, she could not speak. She thought she must look to Ken like some submarine creature that had been thrown onto dry land and lay gasping.

Ken walked slowly toward the bed.

"Here," he said, taking the earring from her hand. "Allow me." His tone was more than solicitous; it was gallant. And, holding her earlobe steady with one hand, he passed the wire through her flesh with a single quick movement. Rosalie felt the casual dexterity of his touch spread from her ear to her neck, then across her cheek until her whole body shivered in the warmth of it. At the same time she saw his large shadow fall across her body. The weight of it made her gasp.

The visit was virtually mute, as though the passage of the earring had left them spent, in no need of speech. Ken sat stiffly upright in a ladder-back chair he had drawn up to the bedside. Rosalie watched him in silence for a few minutes before submerging into sleep. Now and then her pupils would appear beneath half-open lids. Ken watched them struggle to focus upon him, then rove upward behind half-drawn lids, leaving only the white lunar rims of blindness. At last, he rose, steadying the chair lest it scrape against the floor and awaken her. Then turned, and without a backward glance, left the room. Rosalie did not awaken.

When, later, Anna arrived, it was to find her mother deep in coma. From the corridor, she had heard a moist bubbling sound. What she saw when she opened the door was a tiny snout poking through an abandoned nest of gray hair. With each shudder of the chest, gold earrings shook off a tiny brave flash. Anna sat in the chair that Ken had earlier that day occupied. An hour later she saw her mother take the last of many deep breaths, deeper than all the others, and slowly deflate into death. A nurse entered, closed her mother's eyes with her fingers and bound up the fallen jaw with a gauze bandage. To Anna, who watched, it seemed that in that pinched mouth and closed lids, the passion expressed itself all the more; sealed now within her mother's body, it would live on long after she had died.

"Poor woman," said the nurse.

"No," said Anna. "You are quite, quite mistaken."

How to Build a Slaughterhouse

It is May and, for whatever reason, I have been invited to serve on a jury that is to pass judgment on the final projects of a group of candidates for the degree of Master of Architecture at Yale University. But I am not an architect. I am a surgeon. Nor do I know the least thing about buildings, only that, like humans, they are testy, compliant, congenial, impertinent. That sort of thing. When I am faced with blueprints and drawings-to-scale, which are the lingua franca of architecture, something awful happens to the left half of my brain. It shrinks, or dessicates, collapses, and I fall into a state of torpor no less profound than that of the Andean hummingbird when it is confronted with mortal danger. Sadly, my acceptance of such an invitation by the Yale School of Architecture is just another example of the kind of imposturage of which otherwise honest men and women are capable.

The charge that has been given the students is to design and build an abattoir. It is understood that prior to this undertaking they have, as a class, made a field trip to a slaughterhouse in the New Haven area. For months afterward they have been working toward this date. It is two days before we are all to meet for the examination in the seventh floor "pit" at the School of Architecture. But if I cannot know what they know of buildings, at least I can have seen what they have seen, and so I telephone the owner of the slaughterhouse on the outskirts of New Haven, the one that the students visited months before. "Yes," he says, "by all means." His voice is genial, welcoming.

It will be no great shock, I think. A surgeon has grown accustomed to primordial dramas, organic events involving flesh, blood, and violence. But before it is done this field trip to a slaughterhouse will have become for me a descent into Hades, a vision of life that perhaps it would have been better never to know.

In a way, it is the last place on earth that seems appropriate to the mass slaying of creatures. Just another grinding truck stop off Route 1 in North Haven, Connecticut, with easy access for large vehicles and, nearby, an old cemetery tossing in the slow upheaval of resurrection. It is 7:00 A.M. Outside, another truck rumbles into the corral.

THERMOKING is the word painted on both sides of the huge open-sided car filled with cattle. Each cow has a numbered tag punched through an ear. Outside, the enclosure is already ridiculous with lambs. What a sinister probability this truck gives out. Inside it, the cows are, for the most part, silent until one lifts its head and moos wildly. Now another joins in, and another, until the whole compound resounds with the terrible vocabulary of premonition.

The building itself is low and squat—a single story only, made of cement blocks and corrugated metal and pre-stressed concrete. Behind it is a huge corral. Such a building does not command but neither does it skulk. It carries out its business in secret and decides what you will see, hides from you what it chooses. If only I can come upon it—the undiscovered heart of this place that I know, must

believe, is here. Does this building breathe? Has it a pulse?
It must.

Now the gate at the rear of the truck is opened. The
cattle mill about like bewildered children until, prodded
from behind, they move sightless and will-less down the
ramp and into a gated pen as if in sleep through an incurable dream. Here they come, slowly, their hooves
weighted down with reluctance. The wooden floor of the
entryway is scarred, packed and beaten. The hooves, stag-
gering, thump the timbers. There is a quick lateral skid
on manure. It is the sound of those skidding hooves that,
months later, you will hear while waiting in line at the bank
or getting a haircut.

The cowherd urges them on. They seem afraid of dis-
pleasing him. With gentle callings and whistles he inveigles
them into the pen. I keep my gaze on a pair of mourning
doves waddling among the droppings until, threatened by
a hoof, one takes to the air with a muted small whistling
of its wings. The other follows in a moment. Against a
nearby fence a row of fiery tulips spurts. Into the narrow
passageway the cattle go single file, crowding at the mouth
of it, bumping into each other, clopping sidewise so as not
to lose their place. It's as if, once having passed through
that gate, they would be safe. As if what lay ahead were
not extinction but respite, and there were not, just ahead,
death bobbing like clover in a pasture, but life. Only the
first two or three begin to suspect. One after the other
these lift their heads at the sound of the stunning gun. But
there is the sweet assuaging voice of the cowherd and the
laughter of the men inside to draw them on.

The one at the van shies as she encounters some hard
evidence. She balks, stops, the others press against her
until, with a toss of her horns, she throws her new knowledge down before the herd, like an impediment. Without
warning (do I imagine it?) the leaves on the trees at the

periphery of the corral begin to siffle, the grass to stir. Tails rise as if in a wind. Ears and flanks shiver in a cold blast. As abruptly, all is still. But I see it has not been the wind, only death that has swept across the corral and whooshed away.

Inside, the men are waiting. All are dressed in identical uniforms—overalls, ankle-length rubber aprons, high rubber boots and orange plastic hard hats. The hooks, tracks, scales, tables and trays have an air of brutal metallic strength; there are no windows nor anything made of wood. The room echoes like a gymnasium. From somewhere too far off to be heard clearly, a silken radio voice announces the morning news. Something about a famine in Ethiopia . . . There is the smell of cowhide and tobacco. One of the men clicks over the multitude in the pen. ". . . six, eight, ten, fourteen . . ." he counts. "Plus one hundred sixty. Jesus! a day's work."

The Process begins. There is a muffled whump from the stunning pen, like the firing of a mortar shell. A body arches, the tail blown forward between quivering legs. She goes down, folding on all fours at once, something from which the air has been let out. They drag her a foot or two to the hoist. A chain is placed about one hind leg and the winch activated. A moment later she is aloft above the Killing Oval—a kind of theater with a centrally slanting stone floor and a drain at the lowest point. As she hangs upside down, her coat seems a bit loose, shabby, with all the points and angles of her skeleton showing. The throat slitter is ready. It is clear that he is the star. Enisled in his oval space, alone there with his cattle who, one at a time, stretch out their necks to him, he shines beneath his hard hat. He is blond; his eyes blue knife blades; hefty; a side of beef himself, though not at all fat. No part of him shakes with the thrust. Still, if physiognomy is any hint of character, he has found his rightful place. The eyes boil from her head; saliva drips from her limp tongue. Up on his toes for the sticking, and oh those chicory-blue eyes. For just so long as the blade needs to burrow into the neck— one second, two—the pudgy hand of the man grasps the ear of the cow, then lets go. He is quick with the knife, like a robin beaking a worm from the ground. The slit is made just beneath the mandible, the knife moved forward and back and withdrawn. In this manner the jugular vein and carotid artery are severed. The larynx, too, is cut through. He has a kind of genius. His movements are streamlined, with no doubt about them. How different from my own surgery where no single move but is plucked at by hesitation.

In the abattoir there is gradation of rank, at the bottom of which hierarchy is the hoser, often the newest member of the group. Only after a long education to the hose will he be formally instructed in the art of stunning and hoisting. Then on to bunging, decapitation, amputation of the hooves, gutting, skinning, and, if his dream is to be realized, killing, which is at the pinnacle. In this, it is not unlike the surgical residency training program at Yale. Never mind.

The stunner turns their brains off like spigots; the slit- ter turns on the faucet of their blood which squirts in a forceful splash toward the stone floor. For a moment the cows are still, megaliths, then a mooing, flailing, kicking as the effect of the stunning wears off. Now and then the slitter must step out of the way of a frantic hoof. It takes so long until all movement stops! As the bleeding slackens the hose is used and the business dilutes into wateriness. The hose flogs across unblinking eyes; it is a storm of weeping. I am tempted to reach out, I am that close, and lift a velvet lip, finger a horn, but I do not. There is rebuke implicit in such acts.

"Two hundred and fifty gallons of water per second,"

the hoser tells me. It does not occur to me to doubt him. I peer through the scrim of blood and water to the stunning pen where the next cow has just been felled. It is in the stunning pen that the animals seem most exposed, with no tiny shield of leaves, no small tangle of brambles, such as any captured thing is entitled to hide behind. And all the while the flat mooing of the already-slit, a hollow blare pulled up and out from their cavernous insides that stops abruptly and has no echo. And the howl of the stunned. Now there is a throatful of hot vowel if ever you heard it.

Each cow is impaled at the groin on a ceiling hook and detached from the hoist to make room for the next. These ceiling hooks are on tracks and can be pushed along from station to station. A second hook is used in the other groin. A light touch sends the splayed animal sliding on the rack like a coat in a factory. Already there is a second cow bleeding from the hoist, and the third has been stunned. The efficiency of the men is a glittering, wicked thing. They are synchronous as dancers and for the most part as silent. It is their knives that converse, gossip, press each other along. The smallest faltering of one would be felt at once by each of the others. There would be that slackening which the rest would have to take up. But now and then they laugh, always at each other, something one of them has said. One of them is always the butt. It does you good to hear this chaffing. I see that without laughter the thing could not be done. They are full of merriment, like boys. Or like gods, creating pain and mirth at the same time. A dozen times a day, the hoser, who is younger than the rest and a little simple, I am told, turns his hose on one of the other men who roars with outrage. Everyone else dies of laughter, then rises again, redder in the face. What are their minds like? Bright and light and shadowless, I think. Disinfected.

There is a sequence to it: stun, hoist, slit, hose, bung,

behead, amputate and gut. Each step in the process is carried out by one man at his station. The cattle are slid from one to the other on the racks. What a heat! What an uproar! Already the sink and scales, all the ghastly furniture of this place retreats into far corners and I see nothing but the cattle. At one end of the room the heads are lined up on a folding rack, such as might otherwise be used to dry clothes. Tranquillity has been molded into their mouths. The once swiveling lips are still; the brown eyes opaque. Here they are axed open and the brains examined by the inspector.

"What are you looking for?" I ask him. With scissors and forceps he cuts into the base of one brain.

"Pus, spots, lumps," he says. I peer over his shoulder and see instead at the back of the cow's eyes all the black and white of her tribe puddled there. At the base of her brain a sloping pasture, green with, here and there, a savory buttercup to which all of her life she had lowered her muzzle. And in her throat, pockets of retained lowing which I think to hear escaping even as he prods the tissue with his forceps.

The beheader is not yet twenty. When he turns to see who is spying there, his smile is hesitant and shy. Around his waist a chain belt holds a bone-handled sharpener and a spare knife. He flashes his wrist and there is the quick hiss of the blade against the rasp. Later he will show me his knife, let me heft it, turn, flip, feint.

"Nice?" he asks me.

"Nice," I say. "Nice." Abruptly, he kneels to his work. He might be giving first aid to the victim of an accident. Not Judith at the nape of Holofernes nor Salome working her way through the gorge of John the Baptist was more avid than this youth who crouches over his meat like a lion, his blade drinking up blood.

The first slitter has been replaced by another. This one

is Italian. His hair is thick and black with just a spot of russet like the flash of a fox's tail. His shoulder is jaunty, his cheek shadowed by eyelashes as he sinks the knife. It is less a stab than a gesture, delicate and powerful, the thrust of a toreador. Against the tang of his knife, the loaded artery pops, and the whole of the cow's blood chases the blade from the premises. I see the slow wavelike pulse of the slitter's jugular vein. Once he laughs out loud. The sound is sudden and unexpected. I turn to watch the mirth emerging from so much beauty of lips and teeth and throat. At eye level a posthumous hoof flexes, extends, flexes again.

All at once, a calf, thinking, I suppose, to escape, wallops through the half-open gate of the stunning pen and directly into the Killing Oval. She is struck on the flank by a bloodfall from the hoist. Her eyes are shining pits of fear. The men view this with utmost seriousness. Immediately two of them leave their tasks and go to capture the miscreant, one by the tail, the other by an always handy ear, and they wrestle the calf back into the pen to wait her turn. Now here is no Cretan bull dance with naked youths propelled by the power of horns, but an awkward graceless show, as the calf robs them of their dignity. They slide on the floor, lose their balance. At last calm is restored. Half an hour later, writhen and giving up the ghost, the calf has her turn. So, there is a predetermined schedule, an immutable order. Why?

". . . nine, ten, eleven, twelve. One dozen." Someone is counting a cluster of impaled and hanging calves. They are like black-and-white curtains ungirt, serious. The men part them with the backs of their hands in order to pass through. They are not just dead; they are more than dead, as though never alive. Beyond, trays of steaming guts; another rack of heads, all clot and teeth. Each head is tagged with the number of its carcass, just so each plastic bag of viscera. Should a beast be found diseased in any part, the inspector discards the whole of it. The men do not wear gloves but plunge boldly into the swim. Are they in a kind of stupor of blood? Oddly spellbound by the repetition of their acts? Perhaps it is the efficiency of the Process which blinds them. I think of the wardens of Auschwitz. At the final station, barrels of pelts. For leather, for rugs.

"A guy in New Jersey buys them," the skinner tells me.

I see that one of the slit and hoisted continues to writhe, and all at once she gives a moo less through her clotted muzzle than from the gash in her neck. It is a soft call straight to my heart. And followed by little thirsty whispers.

"It's still mooing," I say.

"Oh, that," says the slitter.

"How can that be?" I ask. "The larynx has been severed. Hear that?" He cocks his head. There is a soft sucking sigh from the veal cluster farther on, as though someone were turning over in his sleep.

"They do that sometimes," he explains, "even that long after they've been cut." There is an absolute absence of any madness in him which might explain, mollify, soften. He is entirely cool, reserved, intent.

But today they have not been able to kill them all. Some will have to wait overnight in the corral. Thirty minutes after the command has been given to stop, everything in the slaughterhouse is neat and tidy, as much as rinsing and scrubbing can make it so. The tools have been scraped clean; the planks scoured and freshly swept. When it is all done, the beheader snatches a hose from the youngest, the one who is simple, and sprays him in the crotch. Another joins in the play. How young even the older ones look now. They are eager to go home, where I should think them the gentlest of men. This slaughterhouse is a place one leaves wanting only to make love. In the courtyard my nose is feathered by the smell of fresh air. Overhead a gull blows by, beaking at the sky. From my car I see a cow swing her muzzle at a fly, lash with her tail and fall still. On the roof, along the eaves, doves mourn.

In the morning I arrive just before the men. I wait for them to come. Soon they do. One of them has brought a little dog, a terrier, who scampers along, bouncing sideways and snapping high-pitched chunks out of the silent air. The sight of the dog tickles the men, each of whom stops to pet or scratch. "You, Fritzie," they say, and growl, "little pecker." Now the building awakens, accepting clatter and water gushing into its basins. It begins again.

For two days my new colleagues and I watch and listen as the twelve students present their models, their blueprints. Never, never have there been abattoirs more clever, more ingenious than the abattoirs of Yale. For ease of access the "Plants" are unequaled. Railroad sidings, refrigerated trucks contiguous at one end, attached meat markets. It is all there. And inside, disposable plastic troughs for collecting the blood, fluorescent lighting, air purification, marvelously efficient stunning rooms. "Here," they say, pointing, "is where they are stunned." And, "I have placed the killing alcove here." The faces of the students do not change; they do not tremble at the reenactment of Purgatory. Rather, a cool, calm correctness is what they own. Like the slaughterers, the students have grown used to the awful facts; what concerns them is the efficiency of the process. When they speak of the butchers, they commend their technique. And so do I. So do I. And if ever I should wish to own an abattoir, I would be wise to choose any one of these student architects to make it for me. But there is another abattoir that concerns me now. It is the real abattoir that lies just beneath the abattoir these architects and I have seen.

• • •

In the design and building of an abattoir one must remember that once it was that the animals were the gods. Slaughtering was then no mere step in the business of meat preparation but an act charged with religious import and carried out in a temple. The altar was sprinkled with blood. The flame of animal life partook of the sacred and could be extinguished only by the sanction of religion. But, you say, what can architecture do in the face of slaughter? Beauty and spirit stop at the first splash of blood. Better to settle for efficiency. But efficiency gives way before the power of the mythic imagination. And so we shall try:

First, the location. No grinding truck stop on the highway, but a cool glade at the foot of a ridge with, beyond, another ridge and another. Some place beautifully remote, I think, on a small elevation from which the sky and the sun might be consulted. Yet not so high as to be seen silhouetted against heaven from the sea. That is for temples and lighthouses. Nor ought it to be easily seen from any road but must be out of sight, like certain sanatoria, oracular pools, surgical operating rooms. A place without vista, turned in upon itself. And hidden by trees. The gods always play where there are trees that invite mist to their branches. I should build it in a grove, then, to benefit from the resident auspicious deities. And yes, trees, not so much to lend mystery and darkness as for companionship, to bear witness. Let a vivid spring leap nearby with water that is cold and delicious. To listen to its quick current is tantamount to bathing in its waters. Just so simply are ablutions performed. Hand-scooped from the stream, such water will, if drunk at certain susceptible times of the day—twilight and dawn—summon visitations, induce dreams. Pulled up into the throats of the doomed beasts, it will offer them peace, make them ready.

At this place let there be equal parts of sun and shade and at night the cold exaltation, the lambent flood of moonlight. And no nearby houses, for the shadow of this place must not fall across the dwellings of human beings. Killing of any kind has its contagious aspects. Place it thus and the abattoir becomes a god—distant, dignified, lofty, silent. Gaunt and stark until the beasts are ushered in. Only then does its blood begin to flow. Only then is the building warmed and colored, completed. Made human. Such a building is a presence. I would want anyone looking at my abattoir for the first time to fall under its spell, to believe it particularly his as well—there would be that certain tilt of a roof, the phantom shadow of leaves cruising over tile. One glance at such a site and you will say as Oedipus said at Colonus: "As for this place, it is clearly a holy one."

David, it is reported in the Bible, purchased a threshing floor from Araunah the Jebusite upon which to build the altar of his temple. Alas, the Jebusites are no more, and neither are their threshing floors to be found in the land. Even so, I would use stone for the floor, roughhewn granite quarried nearby, granite that will wash black in the rain, turn gold in the setting sun. Granite with beveled edges cut to fit neatly, the gaps between to be filled with mortar. Brick too is permissible since the elements of earth and fire are combined to form it. Brick is earth which has gone through fire. It is sacrificial. None of this will be understood by those who see but a stone in a stone, a brick in a brick. It is in the precise placement and the relationship of these materials that their sacramental quality lies. The roofs of the inner passageway will be of slate raftered with the bisected trunks of oak trees upon which strips of bark have been left. These trees should be felled in October, for in the spring all of the power of the tree is devoted to the making of leaves. In the fall the wood is more compressed and solidified. Oak is preferred above all others, as much for its strength and resistance to water as for the news whispered by its leaves that nothing is annihilated; there is only change and the return of matter to a former state. Stone, brick and wood, then. The earth has been burnt; the stone has been cut from its place; the tree has been felled; and all three rise in the form of the abattoir. Yet their texture must survive. The memory of the original tree, clay, earth, stone, is made permanent by the form in which each is made. The builder with his hand and his eyes must do justice to the talent and potential of the material. Nor are these materials passive but offer their own obstacles and tendencies.

Centrally, there is to be a vast open atrium flanked by columns whose capitals are carved as the horned heads of beasts. Everything must reflect the cattle. They are the beating heart of the place. So let there be columns and an unroofed atrium. As nobody can live without the ample to-and-fro of air, so will the building be dead that does not permit the internal play of abundant air. Between the columns of the atrium place lustral stone basins in which water from the stream may be collected for the washing of hands. Columns too, for avenues of light that in the company of the breeze and the high fountain will rinse the air of reek.

The building faces east to receive the morning sun in which it is best for the men to work. There are to be no steps in any part of the abattoir, only timbered ramps curved like those of a ziggurat along which the animals are led up to the porch or vestibule. This antechamber measures in cubits twenty by twenty. (The cubit being the length of the forearm from elbow to fingertips.) It is the function of this room to separate the profane world from the sacred area which is the atrium. In order to enter the atrium the cattle must pass in single file beneath an arch. It is well known that to pass through an archway is to be changed forever in some way. Who is to say that such a passage does not purify these beasts, make them ready to die? The atrium itself is vast, measuring in cubits sixty long, forty wide, and thirty high. As I have said, it is roofless in order to receive the direct rays of the sun. Nor has it any walls on either side but open colonnades. To the rear of the atrium is a third and smaller room where the men take their rest. Inside, the corridors, vestibule and resting room must be brilliant with light from wall lamps and skylights. Shadows are dangerous in an abattoir. They make you think. There is to be no rebirth here, as we know it. It is a place for endings, where residue is hosed away and no decay permitted.

Let us dwell upon the interior of the building. If a stable has the odor of manure, why, that is fitting to the stable. The smell increases the stableness of the building, confirms it in its role as the dwelling place for beasts. Just so is the odor of fresh-spilled blood apt for an abattoir. You would not expect perfume. Still, I would be grateful for the sacred smell of sawdust or straw—for the sake of the cattle, to conceal it from them. Blood has no smell, you say? And it is true that there is no odor of it in the operating room. But I think that to catch the whiff of blood is a talent beyond human olfaction. Tigers smell blood and hunt it down precisely. And sharks who, having shed a single drop of their own blood, will devour themselves. Are you certain that domestication blunts the noses of these animals? No, compassion dictates that we separate the about-to-be-slain from those crossing over. Listen! The stones ring with hooves. And in a corner of the atrium, the sawdust is roiled where one of them has floundered, the cloven hoofprints brimming with red shavings. And no reek in the air.

When, as happens, they cannot all be slain in one day,

the cattle are led at dusk from the clearing in front of the abattoir down to a narrow tortuous path lined by thick shrubbery. It is the same path by which they left the world at dawn. Here and there the path forks, suggesting a labyrinth. Such a serpiginous route emphasizes the immense apartness of the abattoir. They are ushered into a pasture at some remove where they spend the night in a world cast in frost and moonlight. Stay with them through these hallucinated hours white as foam and filled with heightened meaning. Be there just before dawn, waiting. Long before you see them you will hear the sound of their lips pulling at the grass of the pasture. Ah, there! Look! The first one—all white, breasting the mist, then coming clear of it, like a nymph stepping out of the woods.

Now they are led back to the slaughterhouse. I hear the soothing murmur of the herder making his sweet deceit. "Come along now, ladies. Be polite. No need to crowd. It's all the same in the end." A moo interrupts.

"Hush, now." Again the labyrinthine path must be navigated. In the early morning the climate of the place is that of a cellar—cool and cavernous. There are the pillars caught in the very act of rising. There is the sibilance of insects and a throbbing of frogs. The mist rises and soon there are drifting veils of water and sunlight, something piney in the air. Pious the feet that pace the stone floor of the atrium. The heads of the men are covered with small capulets. Prayers are recited. One of them holds the knife up to the sunlight, then turns to examine its larger shadow upon the floor. Any nick or imperfection that might cause suffering to the animal is thereby magnified and corrected before the beast is led to it. At the last moment the blade is smeared with honey for sweetness and lubrication. All the energy of the place emanates from the edge of that knife blade. It is a holy object, a radiant thing. In the dazzling sunlight it is like a silver thorn to be laid upon the willing neck of the beast.

But a cow is not much, you argue. A cow is not beautiful as a trout, say, is beautiful. A trout—made of river water, and speckled stone, and tinted by the setting sun. Nor are cows rare, as peacocks are rare, or certain blue butterflies. These cattle bring with them no paraphernalia of the past. They have none. I tell myself that. For a cow, the sun that rises each day is a brand-new sun, not the one that set the day before and rose the day before that. Humans are the only ones afflicted with a past. But then I think of the many-cattled pastures of my childhood in the milk-drenched upper counties of New York State. I close my eyes and see again a herd upon a green slope. There! One lifts her dripping muzzle to stare at a trusted human being. Nonsense, you say, to deplore this slaughter when with each footstep we erase whole histories. Besides, they do it humanely. What! Would you rescue them? Burst upon the scene with a machine gun and order the animals to be loaded on the truck and driven away? To the country, to the middle of the meadow, and set them free?

I know, I know. But to one who watches from the periphery, there seems no place for this event in human experience.

Hypocrite, you say, why don't you give up meat instead of professing all this outrage?

Give up meat! Oh, no, I couldn't do that, I have eaten meat all of my life. Besides, vegetarianism seems to me a kind of national atonement, an act of asceticism like the fasting that is done during Lent or on Yom Kippur.

So. We are all meat eaters here. The desire for meat is too deeply seated in us. As deeply seated as the desire for romance. The difference between those butchers and you is that they do not come to the abattoir each day with their hearts gone fluid with emotion. They have no patience with the duplicity of sentiment.

It is the next day, and already the event is too far away for grief or pity. How quickly the horror recedes. I pass the butcher shop whose window is neatly arranged with parts of meat labeled shank, loin, T-bone. For a long time I stand gazing at the display. For one fleeting instant it occurs to me that this window full of meat is less than dead, that, at a given signal, the cut-up flesh could cast off its labels and cellophane wrappers and reassemble, seek out its head and hooves, fill with blood and *be* again. But the thought passes quickly as it came.

"Is the veal fresh?" I ask the butcher.

Slaughtered yesterday," the man says. "Can't be much fresher than that."

"Let me have a pound and a half of the scallopini," I tell him. "Nice and thin, and give it a good pounding."

How to Build a Balcony

Take any gray exterior wall and affix unto its surface two brackets. Upon these brackets lay a ledge. Enclose this ledge with a railing and . . . Presto! the wall springs magically to life. I should think any builder would rejoice to make such a thing. A balcony is a bay window with its shirt off. Reveling in snow, rain, fog and sunshine alike, it is what a window aspires to. Upon such a small shelf which projects from the side of a house, the least object—a pebble, a twig, a leaf—takes on a vast importance. Small though it is, a balcony is boundless, for in all but the floor beneath your feet and the wall of the house, it has dispensed with frontiers. Aboard a balcony you have the sense (it is more than an illusion) that you are aloft and gliding and gifted with grander vision. What a far cry from an airplane, which is technically in the air but inside which vibrating box every intention is that you believe yourself to be on the ground.

A balcony is not a verandah which suggests spaciousness and exhibitionism. One sprawls upon a verandah; one hobnobs with others; one is meant to be seen. A balcony is private; you go there alone; mostly, you are quiet, quiet. Nor do I speak here of those poorer cousins—porch and stoop, whose leaden monosyllables must exist as mere extensions of the house at a level with the ground. It can hardly go unnoticed that the spoken words *porch* and *stoop* are abusive to the mouth for one must keep the lips all but closed while saying them. Each is not so much uttered as spat with a short blast of air. Porch! Stoop! While *baal-ko-kneee* opens the mouth about all three lengths of sound, tonguing them with relish. In the matter of euphony alone *porch* and *stoop* are to *balcony* as sandpaper to silk.

Excluded too are those distant kin—portico and loggia (some say piazza)—which put on grander airs with their roofs and colonnades that do not project from the surface of a building but are incorporated within it. Remember as well that, continued along the entire side of a house, turning a corner even, a balcony becomes something else—a gallery—and may not be thought of here. Most vigorously omitted are the baldacchino and the ciborium. These are no more than ornamental canopies that are either free-standing, project from an inner wall, or are suspended from above and whose function is to accentuate whatever lies beneath—an altar or a seat of honor. No true balcony would settle for the role of ornament. The gazebo and the belvedere disqualify themselves in that they have wandered free of the house and have installed themselves in the garden or upon a hilltop. The solarium is a glass case for the convalescent. Deleted too, the galilee, which, its lovely name notwithstanding, is but an accessory room at the entrance of a church. And equally unacceptable is that bellicose race of barbicans, bartizans, garderobes, parapets and turrets down from which boiling oil is poured and arrows shot. All, all out. What is left is the balcony—that blend of coziness and daring that lies midway between heaven and earth, at the interface of within and without. Only a balcony unfailingly transforms the humblest of dwellings into a mansion.

He who has access to a balcony stands in the entryway of the imagination. He pauses at the window that separates it from the interior of the house, pauses there as at the frontispiece of a book, then steps out and in. Forty-five years ago I knew a balcony that overlooked the Hudson River at Troy. Were I to compare it to anything, it would be to the forecastle of one of the ferryboats that crossed and recrossed many times each day. Only this one bubbled forever on the tide. On more than one sultry night I fell asleep there, awakening to feel the cool touch of moonlight upon my cheek. There too as a boy I have sat at night reading the novels of Rafael Sabatini with a small illicit lamp cutting me off from the rest of the universe. At such times, there was only myself and the page of a book, which is as it should be. A balcony is the only place on earth that I have taken possession of in my own name, seized, and draped my flag across, from then on to be defended to the death.

Forty-five years ago twin rows of balconies turned Federal Street in Troy, New York, into a narrow sea whereon opposing fleets of ships faced each other for the purpose of doing grim battle. So it was that one morning just before dawn in the year 1939, with Europe tottering into real war and the children of the Great Depression besotted with the make-believe of it, I was awakened by my big brother, Billy, with a conspiratorial whisper. It was the morning of the great battle. Pyramids of snowballs had been stacked on balconies up and down the street. Peashooters, some fitted with spitballs and other deadly pellets, had been neatly arranged behind armored balustrades.

Noiseless, Billy and I mounted to the floating bridge of our galleon. From somewhere far below we could hear the grunts of the fettered galley slaves. With what anxious expectation we sniffed for a breeze to set fluttering our standard—a pink pig couchant upon a field of scarlet tulips. The moment was solemn. Through the darkness we could palpate, rather than see, the insolent foe who had claimed dominion over this, our native Federal Street.

Snow began to fall. Huge dry flakes soon coated the deck and further obscured our vision. Still, through the blizzard, we could descry the position and numbers of our enemy. O let me list them: Directly across at 106—the *Michael O'Brien* with a crew of three, the smallest of whom waved and smiled at us before a disciplinary smack from the Golden Duke silenced him. To our right, at 103, the *John Kinnicut* with twin sailors crouched behind a railing across which a blanket had been thrown as a shield. To our left, at 107, the dreaded Amazon frigate *Arakelian* with fierce Lucy and Alice aglare at the helm.

I confess to a moment of terror when I saw the odds against us. I could only hope that they knew as little of naval strategy as my brother and I did. Would high noon see these insolent Spaniards in sole command of our beloved Federal Street with all decency and liberty toppled for ages to come? Still, my heart was gladdened by the sight of our ample store of weaponry and by the sleek, trimmed-down leanness of our ship.

Round and round them we sailed, and soon the air was filled with horrible cries: "Gotcha!" "You're dead!" and "No fair!" Despite the cold, the fight was hot and furious. A storm of shot and shell mingled with the falling snow. Soon the heaving seas were tinged with red.

" 'The multitudinous seas incarnadine . . .' " I said aloud and thrilled at the relevance of literature to life. The vessel of the Amazons was of less effect than the others, due, in large part, to the peculiar manner of their shooting— either underhand or in a graceless sidewise fashion devoid of forward thrust. Whatever the cause, we easily sailed out of their range and again and again drew near enough to tease and maltreat them with our peashooters. Much or all of their powder and shot having been spent to no purpose, the Amazons took to hurling epithets across the waves. The very sound of their maniacal laughter was enough to freeze the heart and melt the intervening snow. All at once there was a terrible sound of smashing glass. One of Billy's salvos had slammed into the left front window of the Kinnicuts' parlor. It was the decisive, nay, the final shot. The surrender of the armada was instantaneous and was followed within two shocked seconds by the disappearance of all of the combatants from the face of the earth. Or sea, if you permit. The passerby, newly come upon the scene, would not have been disputed had he surmised that all involved had perished in the waves. The next day Billy and I claimed victory, but it was, at best, Pyrrhic, since we all—Kinnicuts, O'Briens, Arakelians as well—had to fork over our ten-cent allowances for two months to have the window fixed.

So was fought, and so ended, the Battle of the Balconies. Never since Troy was Troy had so grand a spectacle been seen, so fine a fracas fought. That it proved to be the immediate precursor of World War II serves in retrospect to give the event its full and tragic scope. Who could have foretold the carnage that would follow upon our historic heels?

Time spent alone upon a balcony can be as full of diversion as time spent traveling abroad. What traffic some days! Once, on a balcony in Bellagio, a town on Lake Como, I was visited by the prettiest lizard, shy, modest, yet all in gold lamé. I loved him immediately, especially his erectile neck from which shot glimpses of iridescent blue and ruby. For a long while he sparkled on the railing, then glided down to the floor at the farthest remove from my shoe, about which he maintained a certain prudence. Now he held his nose in the air and his body in one straight line, now his tail was up and pointing. Now he inclined one eye, then the other. At last he darted forward only to draw back, palpitating. When I failed to make the least movement for two or three decades, he rolled the folds of his caparison once, lifted a few gilded scales and plunged into a delirium of green. With a lash of his tail, he was gone.

That same evening a bat scooped by, fluttered to a standstill in midair; about face! . . . and so on to the next mosquito. And one could hardly number the spiders more entrenched between the balusters than I upon the ledge. They lived there; I visited. To live upon a balcony, like a spider, spinning webs of death and beauty, teaching architecture and murder! Why not? If a man can live in a dungeon, he can live on a balcony. The next day a squadron of white moths oscillated between the posts of the railing offering their vast and fragile silence to the spiders and to me. Tomorrow, what? A falcon? An angel treading air? But what is *this*? A team of leaves looping on the edge of an October wind. They gust aboard to snicker in the corners, but not to stay. No broom and dustpan for this crowd. Minutes later, they are again in motion, swirling, gathering to the center, faster, stronger until . . . whoosh . . . and they are gone except for one leaf, still with a hint of red in its dried flesh, now trapped between the bars. I free it with a fingertip and send it off. Always, there is one who struggles to catch up.

The balcony is the chief ganglion of the house. It is not unlike the eye that, in the course of embryonic life, pouches out from the brain and leaves the bony box of the skull in order to live, lidded and lashed, at the surface. Just as it is the eye's task to first see what is outdoors and report this news back to the brain, so does the balcony first perceive, then relay to parlor and kitchen all the sights, sounds and smells of the world. Oh, the things I have seen from a balcony. I have seen a horse strike sparks from the cobblestones as it canters by at night. I have seen, with the first pink of dawn glancing off the roof tiles, a whole city sleeping behind closed shutters. I have watched as the fog turned the yellow lights of the street into bright clumps of mist. I have beheld the silent radiant thing the world becomes under an emerging moon.

One does not age on a balcony, he partakes of time that does not pass, but is always happening, always the same. It is the time of the gods. Only down below does someone shout in anger, a door slam. Only there is the grinding of an overloaded bus, the barking of a dog. On the balcony it is always *now*.

In certain parts of the world, Italy for one, a balcony is not a balcony unless it holds several pots of geraniums and a caged canary. The village of Frazione Sella consists of a single street above which each of the twenty or so houses presents its own balcony with each its own geraniums and its own canary. As the morning sun slowly advances, including first one balcony, then another in its heat and light, each canary, as though following a prompter, begins to sing. To walk the length of Frazione Sella is to be ravished by a ceaseless cascade of trills and roulades. No wonder that Donizetti, Rossini and the rest wrote such sounds down and called it opera. Little credit to them; they could hardly have done anything else. At the end of such a stroll you should not be surprised to find yourself fifty years older, having had all your senses but hearing frozen in time. Here indeed lives joy with a voice beyond singing.

As some would never choose to live without a fireplace, loving as they do the hearth with its whisper and crackle of logs, I shall never willingly live without a balcony. In a house, the opposite of a balcony is a closet, a dark place where things are stored, a place turned in upon itself, into which the smallest shaft of light is an intrusion, something to be resented.

My ideal balcony must be small enough to create the illusion that one is standing in midair. Its balustrade must be made of wrought iron, or carved wood. No other material is permissible. Prestressed concrete, brick or cinder block would sink a balcony, rob it of *ballon*. The best level is at the third story, anything lower being too assailable from the street; anything higher, too remote from it. One must be able to listen to the town breathing below. Too, the third story is high enough to make a mockery of a garden wall behind which one can expect to see all manner of wickedness going on. The railing of my balcony must be waist-high for ease of grasping or leaning. Nor ought it to enclose any furniture save, perhaps, a low stool and a lamp for reading. In the operating room where I work, with the odds mounting redly against me, the image of such a golden balcony can flash at the back of my mind and leave behind a residue of the old calm and perspective.

While some distance from others of its kind is desired, a balcony ought not to be solitary. There is no greater congeniality than two balconies gossiping together above a busy street. But if a balcony must live away from its kind, why let there be a garden below, that the two may beguile each other like lovers who may never touch. In just such a neighborhood, I think to see Juliet step from her window to lean upon the balustrade with a blend of innocence and eroticism.

Yet what an androgynous thing a balcony is, now taking on the forward thrust of power, now acting the cranny where one is tucked and snug. A place halfway to heaven, yet in touch with the earth. Neither indoors, nor out. In a climate of its own. Where the imagination steps off and finds its wings. The balcony is just where the artist belongs.

The Romance of Laundry

It was in a tiny room on the top floor of the Pensione Splendore in the via San Gallo that I had my coming of age. The month was October and, like millions of others, I had traveled to Italy in search of Art and Romance. After two weeks of slouching through the museums and churches of Tuscany I took stock: there had been altogether too much of the former and none of the latter. It was to correct this imbalance that I returned from yet another day at the Uffizi Gallery determined to prowl away the Florentine evening in search of . . . well . . . whatever. Shower and shave having been carried out (how easily one slips into the ablative absolute in Italy), I unzipped my canvas suitcase to take out a clean shirt. An increasingly frantic rummage turned up no clean shirt whatsoever, but a monstrous shirtball—a stiff and yellow wad from which rose a goaty reek and whose many anguished sleeves bespoke a lingering death by asphyxiation.

What to do? I thought. I must go to the store and buy a shirt. But downstairs the *proprietario* informed me that it was a national holiday. The stores were closed. There were violent demonstrations in the streets.

"And the laundress?" I inquired.

"*Impossibile;* the laundress is having a baby."

Now I am nothing if not enterprising and, far from considering my options closed, I noticed that he, the *proprietario*, was approximately my size—give or take an inch in shoulder and paunch. Surely, I thought, this man has an armoire stacked with clean linen. I shall offer to buy one of his shirts.

"My good man," I began and, in that mixture of English, French and Italian by which one fends in those parts, broached the subject. What was my consternation when, having decoded my Babelian tongue, he reacted as though I had made an indecent suggestion. After a rush of what I took to be invective, he became, if not nasty, at least irrational, at last saying, "Why don't you wash one of your own shirts?" With that, he rattled his keys in a threatening manner and turned away.

My glance fell to the shirt he was wearing. Was it just possible, I wondered, that this was one of those occasions when desperate men are driven to strong action? My impulse was to attack and overwhelm him and peel the shirt from his back. But, drawing close, I saw that his linen was scarcely more presentable than my own shirtball. Frayed and rancid it was, with here and there the stain of God-only-knew what ancient sauce. I could not have been more emphatically deterred had I seen rising and settling at an armpit a cloud of tiny winged things. The reader may well imagine with what a dejected spirit I climbed the stairs to my room in the garret of the Pensione Splendore. Splendor, I thought bitterly, and threw myself upon the bed.

Permit me to explain that I was one who had reached almost to the age of prostatism without ever once having washed a shirt. For all those years it had been my principle to understand nothing about matters domestic, of which laundry was but one example. While this was not a condition for which I reproach myself, neither did it give me any pride. Even the language of laundry held for me meanings other than those germane to the subject. *Starch*, for instance, was a synonym for backbone, and both were metaphors for the manly virtue of courage. *Rinse* was a command issued by dentists to mean swish, gargle and expectorate in that precise order. And *blueing* was gerundive, indicating a gradual slide into melancholia. About painting too there were certain things I preferred not to know. Take the meanings of the words *gouache, egg tempera* and *gesso*. Or whether *alizarine red* was pink, crimson or something in between. The consistence of such words in the mouth was sufficient. Let them keep their mysteries. If one were not to be an artist or a loremaster of art, it was wiser to know less than everything about painting. Better to but gaze and surrender. After all, it was the same with love, was it not? Love, in which yards of darkness give just the right penumbra to the incandescent rites.

Besides, in the matter of laundry, someone willing had always been there. As if by magic, each pair of dirty socks and shorts, each soiled shirt and scabrous handkerchief would disappear from my clothes hamper on Friday and reappear in my chifforobe on Tuesday . . . pressed, neatly stacked and with the heavenly aroma of rejuvenation. Now, suddenly, in the Pensione Splendore, in Florence, Italy, there was neither clean shirt nor laundress. What had been a cherished way of life had vanished in the twinkling of an eye.

And so it was that on that October afternoon, for what seemed like hours, I moped and mourned the passing of a happier time until, the poisonous odor from the suitcase having reached the level of visibility, I rose, lurched to the casement windows and flung them open. No sooner had I done so and leaned out to revive myself than my eye was caught by what at first glance seemed the very pennants of glory flapping all about, but which soon revealed itself to be a multitude of gaily colored shirts, socks, shorts and underwear strung on lines from wall to wall above the courtyard below. Still more were draped over window ledges, while beyond the Splendid walls every alley and garden was decked in linen. No tiled roof but was festooned with its flags of red, blue, yellow and white. What a bright *plein-air* look they had, like a regatta in full sail. All at once the Pitti Palace, the Uffizi and those dozens of churches became a chaos of visibilia, giant tombs crammed with static Adams, petrified Eves and genderless angels. So many versions of the kneecaps of God, and somehow none of them right. Better to have averted one's eyes, like the Hebrews, and never to have spoken His name. It was *here,* I thought, here behind the Pensione Splendore where, gay, wild and living, exploded the true, the hidden art of Florence. After weeks of deepening stupefaction at the numberless Annunciations, Baptisms, Last Suppers and Saint Sebastians, I was enchanted. As a field of wildflowers to a hothouse of orchids, so was this backyard to the corridors of the Uffizi. Even as I watched, wisps of vapor were shaken loose from the damp cloth, crystal beads lingered, then fell from the nethermost parts to the garden below.

"Laundry!" I said aloud as though I had just now discovered the genre. Laundry, that lives between memory and anticipation, calling to mind the back which yesterday wore it and the bosom upon which tomorrow it will lie.

"Why don't you wash one of your own shirts?" the *proprietario* had said. And all at once what had seemed a cruel reproach became a trumpeted summons. Yes, I whispered aloud, I will, I will. I returned to that anguish of collars and cuffs I used to call my wardrobe. Not without some difficulty I pried one part loose from the whole, then filled the sink. Seizing the thing by the neck I held it under the water until it was saturated. Slowly it settled, giving off tiny bubbles which clustered, merged, then winked out. Just so, I am told, did the wicked witch in the fairy tale drown a cat. The soap was a cakelet, faintly redolent of lily-of-the-valley. With my left hand supporting the drowned shirt, I rubbed the soap into the cloth first in one place, then another, until the whole of it, armpits, collar, cuffs and all, was treated. All this while, I felt myself to be on the brink of discovery. Having served no apprenticeship, and being wholly in ignorance of the craft, I permitted instinct to lead me along. Holding the shirt aloft, free of the sink and its brine, I seized it with both hands, then dunked and fished, dunked and fished, each time squeezing out the extractable juice. And how to describe the pleasure of the warm soapy water, the slush upon the forearms. Even years later, my mouth waters at the recollection. Now the gloves of soapsuds were peeled from my hands, the stopper was removed from the sink, the grayish brine let go, and the basin washed with clean water. Once again, I replaced the stopper, refilled the sink and the dipping and wringing were repeated until the broth in the sink remained clear, colorless and free of bubbles. With what a sense of expectation I shook out the shirt, flicking open each fold. With nothing short of reverence I carried my work to the window and spread it out upon the ledge. Almost at once I noted that what inside my room had been part of a sodden, inert lump of linen was, out of doors, a dynamic detail in a work of High Laundry.

Was I ever to wash another shirt? I wondered. That was not for me to say. Such matters lay in the laps of the gods. But I had washed *one*, done it once, and to engage in the creation of a single work of art was enough for any man. To have wished for more—a body of work, a whole *oeuvre*—that I left to the egotism and vaulting ambition of daubers, tunesmiths and scribblers. For half an hour I had been totally engaged in the making of art, and I would keep the glory of that next to my heart until the day I died and thereafter.

Many times since in my travels have I gazed from the rear window of a small hotel upon just such a garden of earthly delights as was behind the Pensione Splendore. Just yesterday in the city where I live I turned the corner of a narrow alley and saw a whole clothesline of freshly laundered shirts. One had its tail lowered and its sleeves lifted in the act of taking to the air. One hung stiffly, while its neighbor fluttered and sent its tail streaming. Still another beat its wings to make headway against a breeze. A vigorous blue rowed backward, while a fugitive yellow assumed an attitude of descent as though the next moment would see it alighting upon outstretched limbs. A whole collection of beautiful artifacts of our time. An imperishable document of the fashion of these days. They were the skyiest, the airiest of works, and not at all concerned with death: nothing morbid, no shrouds laid out upon savage rocks; rather a feverish, high-strung, playful gaiety. This is not to say that the tragic sense of life goes unportrayed in The Art of Laundry. I have seen hanging upside down from a window ledge a woman's dress. Pale yellow, I recall, and with its long sleeves straining toward a tiny bathrobe, of the same yellow, which had fallen from that window ledge to lie crumpled upon the walk below. Here was registered simply and without theatricality all the pathos of a mother grieving over the child who has slipped from her grasp. In attendance at the next window a pair of orange socks flickered like vigilant candles while nearby a dozen passionate handkerchiefs, one for each Apostle, wept over the flowerbeds. Here indeed was a museum to which one came for consolation.

Nor is love outside the pale of Hand Laundry. Once,

in a courtyard in Venice, I stood bewitched by the unfath-
omable Giaconda smile of a pair of panties upon whose
fabric all of my life seemed to have been defined, their
sweet transparency made crystalline by the droplets bead-
ing at the crotch. Even as I watched, a pair of male blue
jeans, aided by a gust of wind, had its way, however briefly,
with the panties, then swung off . . . the flirtation being a
perfect blend of tumult and decorum. Pink these panties
were, edged in lace, and with a heart-shaped patch of red
(alizarine?) at the seat. For a moment I felt the lonely
passion of the fetishist. Only an innate sense of propriety
kept me from racing to the clothesline and burying my
face in the panties. Perhaps, I thought, I would return at
night when the sheltering darkness might hide me from
public gaze . . . ? But that way lay madness.

What a far cry from the exhaustion of the Italian Renaissance to the vivacity of Hand Laundry, which is an art
both ancient and modern, independent of history and intelligence. It is a product of pure perception in which suav-
ity and charm give every piece its timeless worth. Here the
undulations of each finished pillowcase are economized
for graceful effect. In the least bandana there is the subtle
suggestion of the human form in all its variety. Nor is there
any crude symbolism in laundry, but something else, something given to work that has not been invented by the artist.
Approach any collection of such pieces. Inhale. And there
rises that mingling of soap, water, air and sunshine that is
the ineffable smell of cleanliness. Sniff an Annunciation
or a Baptism and see what you get . . . dusty nostrils.

The paintings of Tintoretto, Carpaccio and the rest
depend entirely upon what is represented there. Those
painters juxtaposed the sacred and the profane in hopes
of duplicating God's art in nature and in the ways of mankind. They did not know that only anonymous, unsigned

shirts and handkerchiefs and bits of underwear are real, that they alone are capable of expressing the truth. Unsigned, I say, except for the signature of holiness, all traces of the artist having been washed away in the act of creation. Nor is Hand Laundry subject to any restoration save that afforded by simple patch, while on the walls of a thousand churches, all too redly, bluely, and jammed with far too golden a light, Israelites gather manna and Apostles sup for the last time. Of paintings, I much prefer those left unretouched, no matter how severely altered by time. I see no worth in the restoration of old paintings. In the softening of a painting by time there is a natural purpose, offering to what was once gaudy the elegiac beauty of ruins. No, a painting is not finished until nature has had her way with it for a few hundred years. An old painting speaks modestly of its past—everything that it has witnessed and endured. These restorations have all the vulgarity of a dowager having just passed through the hands of her plastic surgeon and beautician. After a face-lift and a henna rinse, what may once have been a fine original has become a pricey reproduction. Is it not part of nature's intent that certain species become extinct, thus enhancing the mystery of the past? I take modest pleasure in the knowledge that hardly anyone would agree with me. But, unlike a novel of ideas, a mere reflection allows one to abandon himself to ignorant candor.

Ah, many the year that has passed, and many the shirt I have washed. But no more. I am far too old and arthritic to lean over a sink. Still, the fruits of my labor have been seen and favored in countless neighborhoods. Students have gathered. A school has been formed. And so it is that for the use and good and profit of anyone who wants to perform Hand Laundry I have set down these remarks and reflections. Let the aspirant make of them what he will. For the *lingua technica* that bears upon such subjects as the making of soap from the fat of beasts, the measurements of the ideal sink, the design and carving of clothespins (Doric, Ionian, Corinthian etc., etc.) and the advantages of water hauled directly from a river or well as opposed to that drawn from a tap . . . for all of this I refer the reader to my manual of instruction: *The Book of Hand Laundry* or, as it is known in the mother tongue, *Lavare i Panni* which, in all humility I place beside the classic *Il Libro dell' Arte* of Cennino Cennini. These pages were not meant for the eyes of that ignorant and swinish bourgeoisie which considers that laundering is a menial task, unfit for genteel hands, beneath its station. Nor were they meant for that horde of blind and rash critics who will take their penny pleasures from loathing my book. "*Cortigliani, vil razza dannata,*" sang the broken-hearted Rigoletto of his tormenters. And he was right. So they are, and so must be ignored lest their aspersions at last turn the launderer murderous. Such perversion of the public taste as is the sole means of their livelihood serves but to reconcile the Hand Launderer to himself.

It is true that there are those who pursue Hand Laundry out of poverty or domestic need. Nor are these to be denigrated, but welcomed without reserve into the fellowship. It is from just such a humble element that many of the great Hand Launderers have sprung. Those who, like myself, out of some misguided and wholly regrettable principle avoided the art for many years are more to be pitied than censured. It should be said at the very beginning that all of these instructions pertain only to the art of Hand Laundry. The modern predilection for washing machines, dryers and detergents is altogether outside the scope of art. Such reductions are hardly likely to shed radiance upon their practitioners. It goes without saying that the grouping of appliances into what is called a "laundromat" is no less than a reenactment of Dante's Inferno. And the less said about it the better.

In all art, great care must be taken in the language used to give instruction in the making of it. Carelessness in the choice of such language implies a corresponding vulgarity of the spirit, and precludes entry into the calling. For instance, *soap* is a noun. The nonwords *soaped* and *soaping*, meant to be verbs, are none such, but bastardizations that serve to degrade the subject. Thus, a dedicated launderer would not say: "Soap up the cloth" but "Rub in sufficient soap so that the material is everywhere seen to be impregnated." That sort of thing. In any case, what is required more than soap and water is enthusiasm, reverence and loftiness of spirit.

In the end you will learn better by seeing it done than by reading. Therefore apprentice yourself to a master for as long as it takes to know these things, at first observing, then performing one by one the steps of the procedure under a kindly but firm gaze. And do not hurry to leave the side of him who instructs you, until he bids you go. Never doubt that he will dispatch you when he sees that you are fully ready.

A few addenda have occurred to me since the publication of the first edition of The Manual. I append them here in all piety:

1. In the washing of small remnants such as handkerchiefs, bandanas or other *pannicelli*, it is best to group three or four of the raglets to provide sufficient bulk that the thumping, squeezing and kneading will not have been delivered against too flimsy a mass. In Hand Laundry, substantiality, remember, invites a corresponding force.

2. Knead the cloth of a shirt as though you were massaging the aching shoulders of one who only yesterday

wore it to work in the fields. Only then will the color truly lighten, grow ever redder, bluer, more white. Grind the heel of the thumb, hereinafter called the thenar eminence, against the still wadded rag, holding the elbow in rigid extension. Lean into the work. A small grunt accompanying each thrust will give emphasis to the task and vent the enthusiasm of the launderer. If one is given to singing or whistling, so much the better, as a melodic line can be punctuated in the precise rhythm of the work. It is well known that the launderer who accompanies his work with song infuses his product with the spirit of that music which attended the act of creation. Thus, should the artist hum a dirge, the laundered shirt, when hung in the back yard, will evoke a sense of regret or loss in the eye of the beholder. Whistle a polka and you give to a pair of washed stockings the jaunty tripping air of a Polish folk dance. The gaze of the viewer will not fail to be infected with such gaiety or sobriety. Personally, I have found the works of Verdi and Donizetti ideal for the laundering of the male shirt. Especially "Ai nostri monti" from *Il Trovatore* and "Tu che a Dio spiegasti l'ali" from *Lucia di Lammermoor*. Wagner, as usual, is unsuitable. Too much Valhalla and not enough oom-pa-pa.

3. In the hanging of the shirt to dry, the master and his pupil must part company. Not even the teacher may dictate to the novice where the washed shirt is to be placed among the other pieces of laundry. It would be arrogant to do so. And far be it from me to quench a vein on fire or pile a heap of stones in the path of invention. For there are no precise rules to be set forth. The possibilities are infinite. Here at last each launderer is thrown upon his own resources, letting naturalness be the single criterion, intuition the sole guide. Consider only that hand laundry, unlike the frescoes of pictorial art, has the further advantage of being movable so that a pair of overalls, say, having

failed to achieve harmony on one clothesline, may be switched to another.

This life of mine is drawing to a close. But, in any life to come I shall once again do Hand Laundry. And should my next batch of children flounder in a braver newer world, searching for some work that will both do good and make beauty, I shall invite them to do Hand Laundry. For it is in the lovely progression from soilage to purity that one locates the dignity of doing for oneself, and the saintliness of doing for others. Godliness, I shall tell them, is next to cleanliness. Long, long ago, I went to Florence in search of Art and Romance. In the simple washing of a shirt I found them both.

A Worm from My Notebook

Were I a professor of the art of writing, I would coax my students to eschew all great and noble concepts—politics, women's liberation or any of the matters that affect society as a whole. There are no "great" subjects for the creative writer; there are only the singular details of a single human life. Just as there are no great subjects, there are no limits to the imagination. Send it off, I would urge my students, to wander into the side trails, the humblest burrows to seek out the exceptional and the mysterious. A doctor/writer is especially blessed in that he walks about all day in the middle of a short story. There comes that moment when he is driven to snatch up a pencil and jot it down. Only, he must take care that the pencil be in flames and that his fingers be burnt in the act. Fine writing can spring from the most surprising sources. Take parasitology, for instance. There is no more compelling drama than the life cycle of *Dracunculus medinensis*, the Guinea worm. Only to tell the story of its life and death is to peel away layers of obscurity, to shed light upon the earth and all of its creatures. That some fifty million of us are even now infested with this worm is of no literary interest whatsoever. Always, it is the affliction of one human being that captures the imagination. So it was with the passion of Jesus Christ; so it is with the infestation of single African man. Shall we write the story together? A Romance of Parasitology? Let me tell you how it goes thus far. I will give you a peek into my notebook where you will see me struggling to set words down on a blank piece of paper. At first whimsically, capriciously, even insincerely. Later, in dead earnest. You will see at precisely what moment the writer ceases to think of his character as an instrument to be manipulated and think of him as someone with whom he has fallen in love. For it is always, must always be, a matter of love.

Let us begin with a man leading his cattle to a wateringhole at the edge of the desert. We shall call him Ibrahim. Shall we locate him in Chad? No, Zaire, I think. For the beauty of the name. Such a word . . . Zaire . . . plays to the savor of the silent reader's speaking tongue. Such a word can, all by itself, sink one into a kind of reverie. Writers must think of such seemingly unimportant attributes as the sound of a written word.

Ibrahim is barefoot and wears a loose earth-colored tunic that flows to his knees. Thin, black, solitary, he walks behind his small herd of cows. Seven. Eight, if you count the calf. For counterpoise, he carries a crook taller than himself with which he poles the sand as he paces. His very stride is ceremonious. Mostly, he is solemn, silent. But at times he sings to the cows until their ears begin to move the better to catch his voice. He knows that they need song to keep going. It is clear that he loves them. Two years ago his wife died in childbirth. Her hands are what he remembers best—what they did to his body: sorted among his hair for lice which they slew between thumb and fingernail with a delicious little click, cleaned out his ears with a piece of straw, smeared him with ornamental paint, and, on the floor of their hut, crept all over him like small playful animals.

At last Ibrahim reaches the wateringhole. Only when his beasts have begun to drink, only then does he think to slake his own thirst. Wading into the pond, he bends to scoop handfuls of water to his mouth. It is a fated moment. For this is no mere water, but water inhabited by the tiny crustacean Cyclops, a microscopic crab with a large and median eye.

Unbeknownst to Ibrahim, Cyclops is harboring within its tiny body the larva of *Dracunculus medinensis*. No sooner does the little worm recognize that it has entered the intestine of a man than it casts off the Cyclops which has been for it foster parent, pantry and taxi, and it migrates into the soft tissues of the man. Shortly thereafter, somewhere inside the flesh of Ibrahim, two worms mate; immediately afterward the male dies.

Time goes by during which the worm within Ibrahim grows to a length of more than two feet and the thickness of a piece of twine. One day, while Ibrahim is squatting by his resting herd, his idle finger perceives the worm as a long undulating ridge just beneath the skin of his abdomen. Again and again he runs his finger up and down the awful ridge, feeling the creature respond with slow pruritic vermiculation. And the face of the man takes on the far-off look of someone deeply, obsessively, in love. With just that magnitude of attention does Ibrahim dote upon the worm. Look at his face! Of what can he be thinking? Of his mother? His childhood? His village? Of the forest spirits with whom he must each day, and many times each day, deal, and whom cajole? At last the spell is broken;

sighing, Ibrahim takes up a small twig and, with his knife, carves a notch in one end.

At the end of a year, the intestine of the worm has shrunk away, and the uterus enlarged to occupy its entire body. It has become a tube filled with embryos. Then comes the day when an instinct, more, a diabolical urge, tells Dracunculus that the hour of its destiny has arrived; it must migrate to the foot of the man. Once having wriggled down the lateral aspect of Ibrahim's left foot midway between the malleolus and the head of the fifth metatarsal bone, the saboteur worm chews a hole from the inside out. Ibrahim feels the pain of the chewing and, peering into the hole, he sees for the first time the head of the worm advance and retreat in accordance with some occult Dracuncular rhythm. And he shudders, for it is with horror that you acknowledge the presence within your body of another creature that has a purpose and a will all its own, that eats your flesh, that you can feel. Feel moving!

Ibrahim does not know that the worm is waiting for water, that only when water covers the hole in his foot will the worm stick out its head and spew the liquid that contains the many hundreds of its get. The worm knows that it would not do to spit its precious upon the dry sand to die aborning. And so it comes to pass that once again Ibrahim has brought his cattle to the wateringhole at the edge of the desert. No sooner has he followed them into the pond than the head of the worm emerges and discharges its milky fluid from the submerged foot. Again the thirsty man stoops to slurp his palmsful of Cyclops and larvae. The cycle begins again.

But now a look of stealth and craft sidles across the otherwise impassive face of Ibrahim. His nostrils dilate, and his face, beneath the high and brilliant sun, seems to generate a kind of black sunshine of its own. Reaching into the folds of his tunic, he brings forth the little notched twig that he had fashioned those many weeks ago. Up till now, he has had the patience of the desert; now he will have the heroism of the leopard. If he has prayed to the Gods, propitiated the Spirits, we do not know it. No amulet swings at his neck. There is only the twig. Hunkering by the side of the pond, one foot in the water, Ibrahim waits. He would wait here for hours, for days, if need be. All, all has been swept aside. Even his beloved cattle are forgotten. There is in the universe only Ibrahim and his Worm. He stares down at his foot as though it were not his own, but a foreign brutish appendage that had been left lying on the desert and that had somehow been woven onto his body, attached there. At last he sees that an inch or two of the preoccupied worm is protruding from his still submerged foot. Darting, he grasps with thumb and forefinger, capturing, and, with all the grace and deftness of a surgeon ligating an artery, he ties the head of the worm in a knot around the notched end of the twig, ties it so that the worm cannot wriggle free.

Very, very slowly, a little each day and for many days, Ibrahim turns the twig which he wears at his ankle like a hideous jewel, winding the worm upon it out of a wisdom that has been passed down to him from the earliest time of mankind, through the voices of nameless ancestors, telling that the truly dangerous is not hard or stony, but soft and wet and delicate. There is no room for rashness. Ibrahim cannot be hasty. Turn the twig too quickly and the worm will break, the retained segment retracts to cause infection, gangrene, death. How dignified the man looks. Each time he squats to turn the twig, then stands up, his full height comes as a fresh surprise to the cattle who lift their horns so that the sun can gild them in celebration.

In just this way, fifteen days go by. At last the whole of the worm is wrapped around the twig. It is dead. Ibrahim is healed.

Now Ibrahim turns his cattle on the long trek toward home. It is hot, hot. The world longs for a breeze, but the winds are all asleep. He feels the desert little by little envelop his solitary body. A vast sand grows even vaster. There is less and less for the cattle to eat. Each year he has had to walk them farther. See how they bob their heads with every step as if they were using them to drag along their bodies. It is true—the desert is spreading—Ibrahim thinks. At the wateringhole the men were speaking of famine. But that is far away, he says. Not here, not in the villages of Zaire. In due time, in due time, the older ones say. Ibrahim feels a vague restlessness, a longing. In three days there will be a feast in his village—the rite of circumcision when the young boys are taken into the adult life of the tribe. An animal will be slaughtered; there will be meat. Should he walk fast or slow? All at once, Ibrahim quickens his pace, calling out to the cattle to move along, hearing already the drums and the singing of the women. He has been away for three full moons. The smells of his village come out to the desert to grab him by the nose, to pull him toward home. Hurry, hurry, Ibrahim! On and on he walks and all the while the space within him where the worm had been was filling up with the music of the feast until now Ibrahim is brimful of it. And he has a moment of intoxication during which he feels the sun pounding him like a drum, and he feels his blood seeping out of the still unhealed hole in his foot to dance about his footsteps in the sand. Then, something stirs in Ibrahim, something, like a sunken branch long trapped beneath the water, bobs to the surface with considerable force. At that moment, Ibrahim decides to take a wife.

• • •

Such, such are the plots of parasitology. Ah, but now you are hooked, aren't you? I have caught you, then? You want me to go on, to write the story of Ibrahim? Well. Where should the story go from here? First to the village, I think, where Ibrahim would join the feast, find a woman with good hands and abundant breasts and make love to her. They would be married. I should like very much to describe the ritual circumcision, the ordeal of the young boys in the jungle, how they are wrapped in the skins of three animals and put in a pit for nine days from which they emerge reborn as men. I should like to render for you the passion of Ibrahim for Ntanga, his new wife, who each night lifts her throat to him for whatever he might wish to do to it; then tell of how, in time, he must once again take his little herd away from the village in search of forage. But now the terrible drought *has* come, the famine as predicted by the men at the wateringhole the year before. The desert itself is undulant, looking most like the water it craves. Ibrahim's skin and hair are soon white with the dust kicked up by the starving cows. He watches the cloud of sand rise and slowly descend. Even the desert wants to leave this place, he thinks. The knives of the sun have split one of his cows in two so that it falls apart before his eyes. Another, the sun has turned into metal. Ibrahim's fingers burst into flames as he grasps a bronze horn to ease the creature's last stumble. Still, on the scabby backs of the others, the white scavenger bird rides. Even that is almost too much for the cattle to carry. He tries singing to them, to offer them syllables of rain, a melody of cool grass, but his tongue is dry. Sand clings to the roof of his mouth. He tries to spit but he cannot. Instead he closes his lips. The last of the cattle dies within three hundred yards of the wateringhole at the edge of the desert. The faithful beast leans against something to break its fall but there is only the air into which it slumps. Ibrahim watches the dying animal collect sand in its mouth, watches death cloud the eyes in which only a short while ago he had delighted to see himself reflected. Now his own body is a knife blade across which, again and again, he draws himself, each time feeling the precise exquisite incision with undiminished pain. Ibrahim staggers on to the wateringhole—three hundred yards, yet a whole day's trek. It is a dry ditch, the bottom fissured. Sinking to his knees, he lowers his head like a cow and licks the clay. Kneeling there alone, his tongue stuck to the baked basin of the hole, Ibrahim hears a muffled clamoring as of a herd far off. A lamentation of hoofbeats and mooing swirls about him. Then all is still. The life cycle of the parasite is broken at last.

The Day of Judgment

Certain occasions do to me what Melancholy did to that youth in Gray's "Elegy in a Country Churchyard": they make me their own. Parades, for one. I have but to stand curbside as uniformed men march by to the music of fife and drum, when a lump rises in my throat and I feel the onrush of tears. A bit embarrassing, considering that everyone else seems to be having fun. What I see there stepping along in more or less precision is not the gang from Hose Company 15, each of whom will go home right afterward to relax with a cold beer. To me they are a squadron of doomed youth heading for some port of embarkation. It's only St. Patrick's Day, a friend says. But it doesn't help. I remain inconsolable. The bones of many, I think, will be left on distant fields. The roses are redder that grow in gardens where young soldiers are buried. Doubtless my reaction to parades has to do with the kind of Civil War songs my mother used to sing at the piano:

> "Just before the battle, Mother,
> I am thinking, dear, of you."

161

TAKING THE WORLD IN FOR REPAIRS

That sort of thing, rendered in her role as the Soubrette of Troy Music Hall, never failed to leave my brother, Billy, and me awash with grief.

It is the same with weddings. Let the first notes of *Lohengrin* sound from the organ loft; let the wedding guests rise and turn to see the bride on the arm of her father, and I dissolve. From then on, it is a matter of hiding the evidence, avoiding disgrace.

"A piss-head, that's you," said Billy. (He had outgrown it.)

Funerals, on the other hand, produce in me none of the expected lugubriosity. Rather, they have always lifted my spirits. Father, who was a wag and a general practitioner in equal proportions, said he liked funerals too as he would take a good laugh over a cry anytime. I attribute my own taste for matters mortuary to Edgar Allan Poe. That single line from "The Raven": "The silken sad uncertain rustling of each purple curtain," when first I heard it read aloud, remains among the half-dozen most thrilling experiences of my life.

It is more than four decades since my ancestors were first settled into the graveyard off Pinewoods Avenue in Troy. I am now a stripling of fifty-six, and four times each year I drive to Troy from New Haven to take my mother up on the cemetery. It is always *up*. I never heard of anyone going *down* on a cemetery. Mother is the last of her generation of Trojans. The others are all long since up there, along with her father and mine. Old as it is, this graveyard has not the grace of age. No shade, no thundering from great trees that might be set off by the wind; only one cranky pine that has kept the shape of the wind, keeps it even when the wind has ceased to blow. Here no moping owl, no ivy-mantled tower. It is a raw adolescent place, a teenage cemetery with awkward tombstones scattered one athwart the other and popping up like acne as though everyone in it had been buried yesterday. And there is something wrong with the drainage. The smallest rainful or the least thaw leaves the paths muddy and rutted for weeks. Be all that as it may, Mother and I, in fair weather as in foul, repair to that bony piece of ground four times a year and, in silence, listen for messages. Memories float from us like mist.

"Here lies . . ." we read, and say to each other: ". . . yes, yes. I know. I know." But for the huddled stones and the absence of a basket, we could be on a picnic.

Try as I might elsewhere to raise the dead, the dead persist in lying with their hands folded. Only here can it be done.

Each time, on the way to Troy, I stop at a roadside stand to buy a flowering plant. I keep a trowel in the glove compartment.

Despite the unprepossessing look of the cemetery, Mother is particular about what goes into the ground.

"Pink! You bought *pink* chrysanthemums? Nobody puts in pink *anything* at a gravesite. It is far too mucosal, as your father would say. Take it back, like a good boy, and get something else, something a bit more osseous. Like white. I'll wait right here. Don't you worry about me." From the car I see her walk up to a tombstone. I see her head nodding, her lips moving. In conversation, not prayer. For Mother, death does not disembody. I return with a pot of yellow chrysanthemums to find her chuckling out loud.

"Something funny about yellow?" I may just get huffy. "They didn't have white."

"It's your father. I was just standing here when all of a sudden I heard his voice telling—at the dinner table, if you please—about the catheter."

"What about the catheter?"

"Well, first he asked you boys if you knew what a cath-

163

eter was, and when you didn't, he told you, all right. A catheter, he said, is a rubber hose you put into somebody's weewee to help them pee if they can't. Why, just this afternoon, he said, I took a catheter out of a lady who didn't need it anymore. She could pee just fine after that.

"Billy and you were spellbound. Billy held on tight to his you know what and said he bet she was one happy lady to get it out of there.

"Certainly was, said Father. Just couldn't stop thanking me. Said I was the best doctor in the world. Madam, I told her (this is your father speaking), you are without peer in all of Troy."

Father had all the wit in the family. Dinners, up to the age of puberty, were one choking spell or food spray after another. Long after Billy and I refused him even our wannest smiles, Father continued to refer to the twin Misses FitzGerald who worked opposite sides of River Street every night as "our Trojan Horse."

"Whoo, she was fat," said Mother.

"Who?"

"Annie Gotshalk over there." She pointed to a place where the turf was heaving so that one stone had settled noticeably. "She's going to sink the whole place yet."

"Fat though she was," I reprove, "her bones lie slender."

"I never liked that kind of talk, and I still don't," said Mother. "It's gloomy."

Last summer I was up there letting my mind drift over the dear familiar scene when all at once I spotted what looked like poison ivy growing right up onto Estelle Silver's gravestone.

"Will you look at that?" I said to Mother. "Poison ivy on Essie's grave. Next time we come I'll bring some garden gloves and pull it out." With an unexpected surge of agility

164

Mother made it over to where I was pointing. I noticed with a pang that she wasn't any taller than the tombstone. She had shrunk that much. Still, she had to bend way down to confirm my diagnosis. Botany is *her* department, thank you. She never trusts anyone else to name a plant. When she straightened, it was to face me at arm's length and tap the air just in front of my nose. She has a certain way with that forefinger.

"Poison ivy it *is*," she said. "And you'll do no such thing." Her voice rang with triumph. "She got just what she deserved. 'Ev'n from the tomb the voice of nature cries,'" sang the Soubrette of Troy, and she did a little step with her toe.

"What's got into you?" I asked.

"That Essie! Meanest woman in all Troy. Heart like a potato. Just ask Rose over there cattycorner." She pointed. "Rose can tell you. Essie was what you call a squelcher. If it hadn't been for her, it would have been that nice Rose who ended up with your cousin Harry. Oh, it's the Day of Judgment, all right."

"De mortuis nil nisi bonum," I murmured.

"I told you once today I didn't like that gloomy talk."

On the way back to the car, Mother and I are given to lingering backward glances.

"Oh, Dick," she says every time. "We've had our best visit yet."

"Yes," I say, "we surely have."

Then she looks at me wistfully.

"You going to come up here after I've crossed over?"

"You kidding?" I say. "I wouldn't miss that show for the world."

Tom and Lily

In the ancient city of Troy (upstate New York, not Asia Minor) in June of the year 1934, a god descended to earth in the guise of a magnificent stallion. Had the people of the town known the true nature of the horse, surely the purpose of His coming would have been beyond their understanding. A banishment, perhaps? A penance? Or to discharge some heavenly errand? But who can know the intentions of the gods? As it was, only one, a sixteen-year-old boy, knew what the horse really was. Of all the Trojans, some fifty thousand of them, it was to Tom Fogarty alone that the truth had been revealed. That is the way with miracles, even those that happen in the midst of a crowd. Perhaps only one person has been made ready to see. Sometimes it is merely a dog that beholds and will wag its tail. Tom himself could not have said what gave it away, what clue. He just knew, that's all.

Since it is not good for even a god to have nothing to do all day, the horse got himself hired to pull one of the bread wagons for Freihofer's Bakery. In those days, bread was delivered. Only the lazy, frivolous or disorganized went to the grocery store where a loaf of bread cost four cents more than if it was brought to your doorstep. The bread wagons had all been painted red and orange. The wooden wheels were black with bright yellow spokes. All of which might have been gaudy except for the word FREIHOFER'S in large black script on either side. FREIHOFER'S was simply not a gaudy word. In Troy, New York, it meant bread.

But in order for there to be a job, there had to be a vacancy. And so it happened that one day Nutty, the dispirited old horse that serviced Fifth Avenue between Jacob and Federal streets where Tom lived, took one last, noisy gulp of water from the trough at the corner of Fifth Avenue and Jacob Street and crumpled to the cobblestones. No amount of nudging, whistling or clicking of the tongue on the part of Hank, the delivery man, could get the old horse to rise again. Like a Mohammedan who has made up his mind to die, Nutty lay with his head on the pedestal of the trough, uncaring what the world did while his back was turned. Three hours later he died. A sanitation truck came with a winch and a pulley and a large canvas harness. Before long, the deceased was swinging in the air behind the truck, all hooves, ears and tail. No sooner had the truck started up Jacob Street hill toward the dump when Nutty slid free of the halter and thumped down with a dead echoless sound. "Machinery," said Tom's mother. "Wouldn't you know. I wish they'd hurry up about it. In this heat . . ."

"What's the weather got to do with it?"

"Nothing. I was just saying . . ."

But Tom knew. The year before, he and his brother, Billy, had watched them fish a man's body out of the river after a week.

In any case, it was Nutty's place that the horse-god took.

Irene Fogarty had had a deep-seated distrust of engines and machinery ever since the old 1921 Hudson broke down on the way from Montreal to New York City and stranded

her "for the rest of my natural life" in this "god-forsaken
hole." Just so had she begun her life of "exile." Her husband, Nathan, who had only the week before graduated
from McGill Medical School, had taken it as a sign. "We'll
stay right here," he had announced. There was hardly any
choice since they hadn't one dollar between them to get
the car fixed and finish the trip. That very day, he had
hung out his shingle at 103 Fifth Avenue between Jacob
and Federal where, according to Irene, she had to live
upstairs from the office and refrain from using the vac-
cuum cleaner from one o'clock to three in the afternoon
and six to eight in the evening, the office hours announced
on the two milk-glass signs in the first-floor windows. What
the Doctor, as she referred to Tom's father, hadn't both-
ered to do, she said, was to take her feelings into consid-
eration, and she had been married to him for barely a
week! By what slender threads we hang, she told everyone
who would stand still long enough, as though she had to
explain why a person like her from a city like Montreal,
Quebec, as she put it, ended up in a place like Troy. She
never should have done it. And *he*, she motioned to the
office downstairs where *he* was sitting in his empty office,
he had absolutely no right. But then, what did she know?
A young girl with no experience. Just *deposited* in this no-
hope town that was jammed with Irish, all of whom were
stone-sucking poor and half of whom had T.B. Not even
the car had been able to pass through Troy without coughing out its last. So that gave you some idea. From then on,
she swore, she would never count on an automobile or any
other mechanical conveyance but would go on her own
two feet wherever they took her and no farther.

Furthermore, it was every bit of two weeks before the
first patient walked into that office, and what was *she* supposed to do in the meantime about groceries and toilet
paper? The patient turned out to be Gertie Rafferty, and

you know what she was. Sixth Avenue with a vengeance. Not that she didn't pity the poor creatures who had to do *it* for a living, but it just showed you what life was going to be like in this rotten town. "What's that woman got?" she had asked the Doctor. She felt she had a right. A rash, he had told her. Judas Priest, she'd said, and that was that.

Day after day, except Sunday, at about ten-thirty in the morning, Freihofer's new horse would turn the corner from Federal Street and start down the block. From his stoop Tom could hear the sound of wooden wheels turning on stone and the spanking of hooves. Clip-clop, clip-clop. Two notes only, always the same but never monotonous. And then the long pause while he waited at the curb. His pace was slow as though he had all eternity to make his rounds. With each stop his load was lightened by a loaf of bread, a dozen poppy seed rolls and, on birthdays, two or three chocolate eclairs. Jacob Street was the end of the line. After the last delivery Hank would click his tongue twice and holler "Giddap," whereupon the horse would break into a canter for the barn, striking a spark when hoof met stone just so.

Wherever he stepped, birds followed. From the distance, his legs were bangled with sparrows, all cheeping for the manure which they knew was there, just within that dark pucker beneath the tail. Back and forth they flew weaving a basket of light and shadow in which to catch the prize. Until, with a ceremonial lift of his tail, he would lay the splendid braided loaf before them. Pandemonium! as they left him to drill into the steaming pile that was not unlike the bread he delivered, golden, and with the grainy scent of meadows. To the birds it was less manure than manna. On those days when he withheld the banquet the bundles of hunger grew reckless and brushed his fetlocks with their wings. Occasionally, a little ball of bone and feather launched itself upward to ride the rump. But that was going too far. One whisk of the tail and . . . back down where he belonged. Little shitpeckers, said Billy, Tom's brother. Once, a marsh hawk, like a flake of soot from a chimney, drifted in from the river, shadowing the sparrows. Suddenly the big bird stooped but the horse had gathered his worshippers beneath his sheltering belly just in time. In a moment the hawk was gone and the refugees were discharged.

Tom could have watched the horse for hours—the way he walked on tiptoe, kicking up mud, dust, leaves but remaining somehow unstained, how he stood motionless at the curb with hooves posed daintily on the cobbles and wearing his head like a trophy or bending to browse among the weeds that flourished in the pavement cracks. Now and then an ear flicked to vent an excess of energy. Once, as he gazed, Tom saw the flesh at one place on the flank twitch to fend off a fly. Once, as he watched, a shiver caressed Tom's belly and he felt his penis grow hard. He sat down quickly and crossed his legs to hide himself. At precisely that moment the horse lowered his own long penis, startling the girlish sparrows who went twittering off.

About a week after His coming, Tom waited until Hank had disappeared into an alleyway with his arms full of loaves, then he walked up to the horse and held out a lump of sugar. There was the soft trembling in his palm, the heat of the breath, those lips that were the velvetiest of his life. He ran his hand down the horse's neck and saw the skin light up the way a carpet will if it is brushed the wrong way. When the horse reared its head and shuddered, Tom was startled. That night, Tom dreamed that he was riding the horse bareback down the block, stopping at each house to toss loaves of bread like alms into doorways. In his dream

170

he arrived at the little square with the horse trough where Nutty had died. The stallion bent to drink. There was a sudden flexing of the hind legs, a powerful thrust and they were aloft. Only then did the horse reveal his great dove-gray wings. Far below lay sooty Troy, coughing in its sleep, with only here and there a reddish light, like a drop of blood. There was the whole night of pasturing among the stars with the back of the horse between his knees and against his buttocks. And at daybreak, the gentle descent to wakefulness.

Tom Fogarty was by far the tallest boy in his class, almost six feet and still only sixteen. His Adam's apple stood forth from his skinny neck like a prow. Erupted, said Irene Fogarty, tearing yet another pair of outgrown pants into dustrags. Why won't he grow out for a change instead of up?

"Can't you find someplace else to park instead of squatting on the front stoop like a gargoyle? Scare the patients to death. That is, if there were any who could pay."

But there wasn't anyplace else to go in Troy in the summer or anything else to do, what with the Depression in full swing. The shirt factory had closed down, and the Watervliet Arsenal. The only thing still going was the coke plant, the drift from which was the reason Irene Fogarty needed so many dustrags. So, in the morning Tom sat on the stoop either alone or with his brother, Billy, just taking things in. In the afternoons Tom walked down Jacob Street to the riverbank. About two hundred yards away through tall grass he came to a small clearing he had made simply by trampling the reeds. It was his secret hideaway. Sometimes he would fish for eels, sometimes peel down and jump in for a swim after which he would lie on his back flattening the reeds still further with his body. The small clearing was partially shaded by a large willow tree that trailed its tendrils in the stream. About twenty-five feet away stood an old pear tree on its last roots. Tom counted six yellow pears scattered among the gnarled and tumorous branches. From where he lay the pear tree resembled a broken chandelier with most of its working parts missing. In the evening the six pears seemed to retain the light long after the sun had gone down. In the growing darkness they looked for all the world like half-trimmed lamps.

It was the twenty-fourth of June. Summer vacation had started three days earlier. Tom, sitting on the stoop of 103 Fifth Avenue, saw, or thought he saw, the curtains moving in the second-story bay window of 104 Fifth Avenue across the street. And behind them, something—a shadow. But that was odd. The only person living there was Maisie Kinnicut and she was at the coke plant. Tom had seen her leave the house himself. The next instant the movement stopped. Whoever it was, if it was anybody at all, had gone, and then Tom wasn't sure. What he had seen was just a pale shape, something wrapped in a sheet, more like a sheet itself with nothing inside. An hour later, when he saw the girl propped up on pillows in the window, it was a moment or two before he grasped that this was, in fact, a person. He asked his mother.

"That's Lily, Mae's niece from Cohoes. She's got T.B. Her mother and father are already both at the San. The girl's going too as soon as they find room for her, poor thing. Has to stay all by herself till Mae gets home from the plant. I think it's terrible. That Maisie Kinnicut, honestly."

"How old is she?"

"I don't know. Fourteen."

"How long she been here? I didn't even see her come."

"A few days is all. She came at night. They carried her upstairs."

"Oh, yeah?" said Tom. "Is she bad?"

"With T.B. there's no such thing as good. You keep away from there, you hear?" She glared out the window. "I don't know what that horse has got against us. He does it right in front of our house every time. Why us, anyway?"

At precisely ten-thirty the next day (it was the hour of the horse), the manure dropped in front of 103 Fifth Avenue where Tom was sitting on the stoop. At just that moment he looked up to see the girl standing in the window of 104. Tom could not have known that for three days Lily had been watching him from behind the curtains, that at ten o'clock each morning she lay in her bed in the bay window listening for the sound of hoofbeats, straining to realize them out of the clatter of the street. When the manure fell, he looked up to see her leaning between the curtains. For a moment their gaze met. When suddenly she laughed and covered her mouth with her hand, Tom felt his face heat up and his chest fill with something he could not hold back until he too laughed and was relieved.

Hank got out of the wagon with three loaves of bread for 104.

"Can I take it up?"

"You want to take it up?"

Tom nodded. "Can I?" Hank gave a quick glance at the bay window but there was no one to be seen.

"Well, sure, O.K. You can if you want to. Thanks. I'll do the first floor."

The door at the head of the landing was half open. Tom knocked softly and entered. There seemed to be no one at home. But he knew that she was there.

He walked through the parlor to the small front room with the bay window. All the houses on the block were laid out exactly the same. It was the pallor of the room that struck him. He had never seen so white a place. A white wicker chair sat by the bed, the posts of which had been painted white. The flowers in the vase were white paper peonies. On the wall, a Japanese mask. The face was chalk white, the hair and lips black. A glass of milk stood on the nightstand. A half-finished puzzle lay on a card table. Completed, it would depict Perseus unchaining Andromeda from the rock. The girl in the bed had a moony ashen look. Her long colorless hair lost itself in the folds of the pillowcase. Even her eyes had been taken possession of by the morning sun. They were crystals of it so that he could not read them. To Tom this room seemed a world of whiteness and silence, a snowstorm. And like a blizzard it was both alluring and inhospitable. It was a room held outside of time, far away from life. Standing just inside the doorway, he felt the menace of the germ-laden air and remembered his mother's words: "You keep away from there, you hear?" It was his first real contact with the disease. Oh, he had known when a neighbor had disappeared or one of the kids at school had failed to show up, he knew where they had gone, that they wouldn't be coming back. He had learned too from his father's talk of patients that he heard at the dinner table. But not like this. Untutored in the ways of illness, he felt dazed and slightly giddy. When, suddenly, she leaned forward and gave a delicate soft bark and he saw the spot of blood on the tissue, he was shocked. All the violence in the world seemed concentrated in that red.

The girl raised the glass of milk to her lips and took a tiny sip.

"Here's your bread," he said lamely. "Hank, the bread man, he said I could bring it."

"No one's here," she said. "My Aunt Mae's at work. She won't get home till five-thirty." Then, remembering. "He's a beautiful horse, isn't he, just the same. I mean even if

174

he does make a mess right in front of the house every day. I couldn't help laughing."

"My mother said he's got a grudge against us. 'Why us?' she says every time." When the girl smiled, he could have fainted.

"My name's Lily."

"I know. I'm Tom."

"What's his name?"

Tom shrugged. "Just Freihofer's horse, I guess."

She sat up suddenly and gave another flannel cough into a tissue, her head turned away from him. He saw that she had been taught to be careful about the direction of her coughing. It was the etiquette of tuberculosis. He recognized it from things his mother had said.

"You're not supposed to be here," she said. "My sputum is positive."

"Hank," he lied. "He said to bring up the bread."

"Still and all you shouldn't. I'm only here until there's a place for me at the Pawling Sanitarium. My mother and father are already there. We all got it. I have to go to the children's ward. I'll be able to see them twice a week. But right now . . ." She gave a sign. "There aren't any beds. I have to wait."

To Tom she was something less substantial than solid flesh. Beneath her eyes, on the prominences of her cheekbones, a circle of dusky red gave evidence of something hectic and ardent. He had never seen anyone so beautiful.

"I have a cavity on the right side," she went on. Tom had no need to ask. Everyone in Troy knew that word. "They tried pneumo on me three times but it didn't work. Pneumo," she said, pronouncing the p, "is no pfun. Now I have to have the thoracoplasty." He saw that she was taking three breaths for every one of his. The spots in her cheeks had brightened.

175

"I better go."

"Will you bring the bread tomorrow?"

Tom shrugged and didn't answer. But he knew that he would.

At dinner Tom asked his father:

"What does it mean when the pneumo doesn't work and they have to do a thoracoplasty?"

"Fine talk at the table," said his mother. "If you don't mind."

"Pneumo means air," said his father. "Thorax means chest. If there is a cavity you inject the air in the space around the lung. This makes the lung collapse so that the cavity will fill up with scar tissue and heal. The idea is to put the lung to rest. But sometimes it doesn't work. Adhesions or whatever. Then you have to take out half a dozen ribs over the place where the cavity is. Then maybe the lung will collapse."

"Will you please?" said his mother.

"What do you look like without those ribs?"

"Caved in. Here." He reached out and touched Tom's chest. The boy flinched as though he had been punched.

"Oh," said Tom and sucked in his saliva. He had an image of her hammered, like a fender.

"Eat your dinner," said his mother. But Tom was already up and gone from the table. He felt their eyes following him out of the kitchen.

The next day Tom came upon Lily sleeping. He stood in the doorway, ill at ease, wondering whether he should stay. Just then the sun slid across the street, probed the wall of the building, searching, and plunged a single ray through the bay window, coloring the face and hands of the girl. At that moment she awakened. It seemed to Tom a resurrection.

176

From then on he came straight to her every day, to that room where Lily too had been waiting for the simple sound of wooden wheels on uneven stone, and the hoofbeats. She would hear Tom's footsteps on the stairs, taking two, sometimes three steps at a time. And always the delicious pause before the click of the door being shut behind him. Sometimes in that long silence while he stood on the landing, when Lily knew he was there, and even afterward when she felt him gazing down at her, she would keep her eyes closed and just listen to the sound of his breathing, the regular slow exquisite sound of warm air passing in and out of him. Each time, she marveled at it. And to Tom, who stood there stricken mute and nerveless, her closed lids and parted lips were an expression of passion so powerful that he would feel a moment or two of dizziness when he would not dare to make a move. He marveled that anyone so free of wounds, so unblemished, so smooth and perfect could be damaged inside where it could not be seen. He didn't believe it.

"You should see my room," he said. "It's a mess. Yours is so neat and tidy, everything in its right place." He thought of the slovenly den he shared with his brother, all their anguished paraphernalia lying wherever it had been kicked or thrown. By all rights it should be his room that was contaminated, not hers.

Tom could not have said when it was that he fell in love with Lily. Perhaps it was the day a ray of sun poked through the gauze of the curtain and roved across her throat. Perhaps it was the time she flirted some crumbs off the coverlet with her long pale fingers.

Day after day he was drawn to that room that only he had the power to set in motion, if only he could find the way to do it, find the part of his body that was the ignition.

In the late afternoon, when he saw the red spots appear on her cheeks and her eyes brighten with fever, he would leave her and go down to the river.

One day, about the middle of August, he noticed that there was only one pear left on the tree. He searched the ground for the others, but they were not to be found. Something took them, thought Tom. A raccoon, probably.

"Brought you a pear," he announced. The night before, he had climbed up and picked it. He polished it on his thigh and presented it with a flourish. Lily raised the pear to her mouth, showing her teeth to it and at the same time glancing up quickly to make sure he was watching. When she bit into the pear, Tom shivered and had to look away.

"Let's do the puzzle," she said. "You work on Androm- eda. I'll finish Perseus." They sat together at the card table, their heads bending close but never touching.

"Hah! Found her knee," said Tom, and tapped the piece into place. "That feel better, Lady?" he said to the half-naked Andromeda still chained to the rock. "Don't mention it, ma'am." Tom could not have known that all the while he was searching among the scattered pieces, Lily, sidelong, had become absorbed in the moisture of his lips, the tiny bubbles of saliva on his teeth that she caught sight of. Once, for an instant, she glimpsed the miracle of his tongue. She made up her mind that it was in his Adam's apple that his soul resided. When he swallowed, the whole mass of cartilage bobbed up to the top, then dropped down abruptly until the next time. Lily half expected to hear a muffled clunk as it hit bottom. It looked painful. Fasci- nated, she waited for him to swallow so that she could see it happen again.

"You're not really trying," he said. "Do I have to do it all?" His gaze followed the pear now decorated with the indentations of her teeth to the nightstand where it rested.

At that moment, he could have savaged the rest of it to the seeds.

"You taking Kinnicut's?" Hank would ask and toss him the loaf of bread. And Tom would climb the narrow curved staircase to the second floor. Sometimes, in the moments before he opened the door, he would hear her singing. It was always so unexpected; and always on those days, she appeared sicker. She seemed to him then like some small nervous creature that emits sounds the echo of which place it in the world. Perhaps, he thought, it was only when the fever rose and she would feel herself floating, only then did she have to sing to keep herself from drifting away for good. Each time, the song ended in a cough.

"You have a pretty voice," he told her.

"I get short of breath."

Tom pulled a harmonica from his back pocket, wiped it back and forth between his lips. "What do you want to hear?" he asked.

"Oh, anything. You pick it." And she settled back upon the pillows to listen, but really she was watching the saddle of freckles across his nose and the way his lips held and brushed the harmonica. She had to close her eyes to hide what threatened to show there.

" 'Santa Lucia,' then, O.K.?" And he worked the harmonica with his mouth, pulling the melody out of it with all the raspy earnestness he could muster, all the while acutely aware of her nipples through her nightgown. Because of that he did not notice the tears on her face until later.

"I always cry when I hear that one," said Lily. "Isn't that stupid? We used to sing it in school every day." But he was not consoled, and cursed himself for making her cry. Nothing works out, he thought.

"Does it hurt?" he asked her.

"Does what hurt?"

"T.B."

"Not really. I don't have any pain. But I can feel it moving inside—like a river."

"I know you're goin' over there all the time," said Billy. "You're gonna catch it in more ways than one."

"You mind your own goddamn business," said Tom.

"Don't say I never warned you."

Irene Fogarty heard through the bedroom door and went downstairs to the office which she never did unless it was something she considered an emergency. She always said that it was in the worst possible taste for a doctor's wife to hang around her husband's office.

"Speak to that boy," she told him. "He's sneaking up to visit that girl at Kinnicut's. She's raising positive sputum."

"Send him down," said the doctor wearily. "I'll talk to him."

"And maybe you should go across the street and have a look at her. It's a scandal the way that child with galloping consumption is left alone all day until Mae Kinnicut gets home from the coke plant. I have half a mind to notify the Board of Health."

Tom stood in front of the desk where his father sat twirling a pencil.

"That is a stupid thing to do," the doctor began. "I thought you were smarter than that. Do you want to end up at the San too?"

The eyes of father and son met. But it was the father who, making discoveries, lowered his gaze first.

"In any case, don't," he said into an ashtray overflowing with cigarette butts.

From then on Tom walked up Federal to Sixth Avenue, then through the alleyway between two houses so he wouldn't be seen. The gate to Kinnicut's backyard was unlocked. He could get to the front hall by climbing into a window. A row of whorehouses occupied one side of Sixth Avenue. Troy was famous for them. The other side of the street was the train station. Every Saturday men came from as far as Hudson and Poughkeepsie to "get their ashes hauled," as Billy put it.

There came the night when Tom, emerging from the alleyway into Sixth Avenue, saw his father come out of one of these houses. Father and son were no more than fifteen feet apart. His father was wearing his gray fedora. A Lucky Strike dangled from his lips. They both stopped dead in their tracks. Nathan Fogarty recovered first.

"Making a house call," he said. "One of the ladies has pneumonia." He saw Tom's gaze lower to his hand where the little black bag should have been but wasn't.

"What are *you* doing on Sixth Avenue?" said his father. "Get back where you belong."

I won't tell, Tom thought. I'll never tell on you.

"Lily?" he called into the room. "It's me, Doctor Fogarty from across the street."

Lily studied the man's face, searching for Tom. All the while he tapped and listened to her chest, she was peeling off the layers of his gray skin, the toothbrush moustache, defleshing the nose, whitening the eyes and teeth, smoothing out the loose folds of the neck that bulged above the collar. But she could find no trace of Tom in this carbon-lipped puffy man. No matter how hard she looked for that bony, lion-haired, hay-scented boy she could not see him. Maybe he takes after his mother, she thought. What she did see in the doctor's face, no matter that he kept it as still as the Japanese mask on the wall, was what she already knew.

"She doesn't stand a chance," said the doctor at the

dinner table. "There's no good lung left. It's the worst kind. Miliary. Spreads through the bloodstream. I don't know what's keeping her going."

"You're crazy," shouted Tom. "Goddamn you!" He was up and out of the house before his mother was sure she had heard what she did.

Now it was the first of September. So soon! School would start the next day. What would happen then? Tom dared not think of it. From the landing he heard her singing, just a few notes at a time separated by long pauses during which she coughed softly. He stood outside the door palming the still-warm loaf of bread. A wave of fear took him. Oh God! What if his father had been right? When at last he opened the door, he was shocked by her appearance. He had never seen her working so hard. Pale as death she lay, one hand trailing over the side of the bed in what might have been languor. With each breath her nostrils flared to open wider the apertures through which air could be drawn. Even the muscles of her neck had joined the battle, sucking in the small hollows there that were wet with perspiration. The muffled coughs were not enough to clear the rattling that slid to and fro deep within her chest.

"Lily?" But she did not turn to see. Tom felt his own chest filling up, congesting. He could hardly breathe himself. He cleared his throat. Twice she closed her mouth to speak, her chin lifting to force a word. "Tom," she managed. He darted to the bed and knelt beside it.

"What?" he begged her. "What is it? What's happening to you?" And he strained to hear, placing his ear next to her mouth. When he touched her, she was like a smooth stone that had spent all day in the sun. Tom had often seen how, after a fit of coughing, her breathing eased and she would be quite composed until the secretions rose again.

"Cough harder," he said. "You got to get it up, Lily. Please cough, Lily. Please." Dropping the bread he seized her floating hand, seized it almost brutally, surely with too much force, and raised it to his lips. That hand, every detail of which he knew, even to the moons of her nails which he had committed to memory. Even now he longed for the private history of each of her fingers, no one of them the same as any other—where they slept, what and whom they had touched. He could have spent his life recording such data.

"I love you," he said. "I love you." It was all he could think to say. Not "with all my heart" or "forever and ever" or any of the tumultuous phrases that swirled inside his mouth. Only "I love you." Those were the only words he knew. He had forgotten all the rest of the language. "I love you," he said again and relished the freedom that the words gave him, the release from all these weeks of restraint. From then on he did not so much bend over her as revolve about her like the sun.

It was his name with which she pulled herself to the surface.

"Tom," she said, her voice whitened by fatigue. "Oh, Tom, raise me up." He knew then that above the tempest of her respirations she had heard him. She had never asked him to do anything for her before, to tend or minister, even on those days when she had been too weak to move from the bed to get something that she needed. Now her asking him to raise her up seemed the most natural thing in the world. They might have been married for years.

He stood then, bending over her, and slid his arm beneath her, feeling for the first time the bones of her back like the wings of a small bird. His own awkward hand was a large and clumsy shovel scooping the girl against his chest. Her hair fell over his arm. For a long time he held her just so, feeling through the thin nightgown the rattling that by all rights should have made the windows shake, the pictures on the walls fall from their hooks.

His arm was heated with her fever. Holding her with her head extended, he watched the wavelike pulse beneath her ear. With every cough she became more beautiful to him. When at last the trace of a smile broke the surface like some rare and beautiful fish, he lowered his mouth to hers. Again and again he wiped the spongy fullness of her lips, playing her with his mouth. There was no going back. Once he had set out in this direction he was unable to stop. They would have one common mouth. He would lick the pain away, suck it from her, find the way to do it, this thing that he had never done before. And so he followed her, breath for breath, drawing in as she exhaled, blowing into her his sweet cool air, pulling out the fever and siphoning off the terrible heat with his own chest. Doctoring her. And himself, too. For this was what he needed in order to survive. And all the while listening to his body ripening, learning what love really was, a contagion. All at once a long soft noise came from her throat, a moaning, entirely distinct from those other terrible sounds. It drove everything else out of range of his hearing and he could only hear that low intoxicated groan into which he plunged and submerged himself.

He was like a conspirator who had at last found the one human being in the world to whom he could pass on his secret, and here he was, whispering it to her, hurrying, desperate lest she leave before he had finished telling her.

Suddenly her breathing quieted, became almost normal. The muscles of her face and neck relaxed, ceased to participate in the violence. He held his own breath in mingled fear and elation. What had happened? Had it passed? Then there would still be time. Oh, please, he thought. Please! Her body which had shaken like a bundle of sticks grew still. All this while Tom continued to fence in her body with his, to cover her with thatch. He would allow nothing in. Let whatever hail or hot ashes fall upon his back, scald or freeze as it would, this, in his arms, would be safe. He inclined his head a fraction down and away from her. When he looked back again he was struck by her calmness. She could not have appeared more composed had she been on her way to church instead of dying, which, all at once, Tom knew she was.

"I'll get my father," he said. And lowered her toward the pillows.

"No," she whispered. "Stay with me. Stay." Her fingertips rose to his face. "You cannot . . ." she began, then faltered. "You cannot love me . . . more than I love you." Her eyes filmed with moisture, grew preternaturally bright.

"I never wanted to go to the San," she whispered, "and have that awful operation. It wouldn't have helped anyway. I'd rather have had you."

"No," cried Tom in a hoarse voice that broke on the single syllable. "No. Don't. Please don't." He shook her against him.

As abruptly as it had let up, the struggle resumed. Already the fleeting momentary smile had drifted from her face. She lay with her eyes closed, not asleep, of course. Acutely awake. Still, he felt excluded. She was dwelling in a place behind her closed lids to which he could not go, nor was he welcome there.

Suddenly she roused herself once more and tried to lift her head in alarm. Had she remembered something that she must tell him?

"Go," she cried in a surprisingly strong voice. "Go away. You must. Don't stay here. Please. Don't watch me. Open the window. Lay me down. Oh . . . go . . . God." Then came the blankness of coma in which the body works long after the mind closes down.

He could not know that what she did not want was for

him to see her die. He had never seen anyone die before. He had told her so himself, once when she had asked. And she had imagined it so many times, the going slack, mouth falling, eyes staring, and worse she was sure, although she didn't really know. Tom lowered Lily to the bed, walked to the door, closed it behind him and crouched on the landing in the posture of vigil that humans assume instinctively, hunkered and with his arms folded about his knees. And he listened to the grating noises that came from the other room, each of which pulled her farther and farther out of his time, his place. She had, with her last words, banished him. He could not go back into that white room into which she had retreated to die. But she had recognized love. He had seen to that. Now when what she asked for was privacy . . . well, he would give her that too.

At five-thirty the noises from the room stopped. At twenty minutes to six, Mae Kinnicut came home from the coke plant. As she rounded the curve in the darkened staircase, she stopped, one foot on the next stair, her hand on the bannister, and stood perfectly still, for she saw him crouched on the landing, and she knew.

"Tom Fogarty," she said quietly, and raced past him into the room. Then Tom heard her wail. "Jesus! Mary! Saint Anthony!" And that awful sobbing. Tom stood and bolted down the stairs and across the street.

"Where've you been all afternoon?" said his mother. "I've needed you to do the garbage cans. Been hollering for you. Can't you hear?" But she stopped when she caught sight of his face and saw the great bereft dumb thing padding across it.

"She's gone then," said his mother, tying her apron and patting the sides of her hair. "I knew it. I knew it. O God, I'm sorry for her and you and everybody in this damn, damn town. I'll be across the street. Don't you dare show up there, you hear? Tom? Tommy?"

She walked to the front door. "May God rest her soul," she said. "The poor little thing never had a chance to live."

Tom said nothing, because he knew that just wasn't so.

Later he saw Lily at Bryce's Funeral Parlor, tiny and mute and drained, a white ash that keeps for a time the shape of the coals from which it has been reduced. He made it out the door of Bryce's and around to the alley before bursting into tears.

The morning after the funeral Tom climbed through the back window of 104 Fifth Avenue as he had done so many times. He had to visit once more that room that all summer long had watched and waited. Every object was there, keeping still its mystery. On the wall at the foot of the bed, the Noh mask, chalk white and with a cowl of straight black hair, shaved eyebrows and open smiling black lips; on the nightstand, the ivory crucifix which time and again he had seen inching toward her fingers, and of which he had been envious, because it, and not he, had enjoyed the stroking of her hand; the vase of paper flowers. Everything watching and waiting as before. Tom thought of Lily's gaze imprisoned within the white walls with only these things for company until the day he had come into the room with love in the shape of a loaf of bread. Even with their terrible permanence, the objects had failed, as he had failed, to hold back dissolution. He would never come to this place again. Tom turned to leave. Just before he did, he lifted Andromeda's knee from the puzzle and slipped it into his pocket.

The next day was Sunday. It had begun to rain—a cold Irish Catholic rain, remorseless and punitive. At exactly ten o'clock Tom heard the bells of St. Patrick's knifing through the streets. A wreath of lilies and gardenias had been nailed to the door of 104 Fifth Avenue. "That's the least she could do," said Irene, referring, Tom supposed, to Mae Kinnicut, whom she felt was somehow to blame. The smell of the flowers permeated the block, infiltrating the alleyways between the houses, coiling and drifting along the gutters, perfuming the brown rainwater that twined downhill toward the river. Tom closed the bay window to barricade himself against the smell; it made him sick, but there was no keeping it out. The sweet odor came through the glass and settled into the lace curtains. He wondered what happened to her germs, whether they died with her or whether, like fleas that leave the carcass of a newly dead animal, they were now roaming the town in search of fresh lung, his own, perhaps, to which with all his heart he had lured them.

"Get dressed, Tom," said his mother, "and shake a leg or we'll be late for mass. I'm really surprised at you."

"I'm not going," said Tom softly. And thought, I'm never going again.

"If you think for one moment . . ." she began, but it was that softness in his voice, she had never heard it before, that kept her from insisting.

"You've grown out of that shirt," she said. "I'll be using it for a dustrag."

A minute later, Tom watched his father, mother and Billy moving through the rain toward St. Patrick's. When he saw them turn right at Jacob Street, he slid down the bannister, took his slicker out of the front-hall closet and slipped into it. At the corner he turned left toward the river. The rain was slanting down harder now. In a minute his hair was saturated. He walked three blocks along River Street until he came to the narrow path that descended to the water's edge, and stood in the little clearing among the cattails that was his place, and his only. This at least had not changed. The same three ducks sat in the water rigid as soldiers. The same willow shed its hair in the stream, carrying in its leaves the same maidenly singing. All at once a wind of its own making flaked the surface of the water. The ducks, disturbed, rose gawkily, flew twenty yards and then came down again, not with any confidence but tripping over the water like skimmed stones, lifting again before settling for good. For a long time Tom stood watching the rain add itself to the river, feeling that it was raining inside his body. Lily, he thought, then said aloud: "Lily, Lily." A single crack of thunder turned up the intensity of the storm, and shutting his eyes against the rain's driving, he headed back home.

By afternoon the rain was smoking all around, an unwholesome gray water that sucked whatever color there was from the town, turning brown as it thickened in the gutters to run down toward the river. But the fall itself was singularly devoid of energy. There was no rebound from the sidewalks, no variation in intensity. It neither waxed nor waned but was of that desolate sameness that wears away the defenses of the mind. It's never going to stop, thought Tom; and he stared down at the street purged of debris and at the rain-beaten cobblestones, each one the blistered face of someone old and crazy.

In the morning he awoke to the drums of rain. Occasionally it would stop to see how much it had already accomplished, then, dissatisfied, would renew itself. During these respites there was a deathly silence while the people waited.

"This town's got nuthin' but weather," said Hank. He was an hour late from having to wrap each loaf in oiled brown paper. "The next thing you know that river'll be givin' us hello right up here on Fifth Avenue. You watch."

Let it, thought Tom. And all at once it was what he wanted more than anything else. By evening the streetlamps illuminated only their own halos. The pace changed. Where before there had been monotony there was now a hectic unpredictability. The wind rose, flinging the rain about. To open the door or window was to breast an element. In the street a bulky shape passed, hidden under a slicker and with an umbrella pulled down about its head, a strange amphibian that neither walked nor swam. Throughout the night and all the next day, Troy sulked. The men got drunker and the women slid further into melancholy. It would never end, they said, never. "Gonna be a flood," they said. And they sat down and waited for it. Even as they spoke, the Hudson River, taking them at their word, heaved itself over its banks.

On the morning of the seventh day, when Tom looked out the bay window, he saw the silver snout of the flood sniffing Reardon's stoop at the end of the block. Moments later the water was dashing to swallow the whole street. One by one the other stoops were lapped. He stared down with momentary excitement. At last, he thought. At last. And he raced downstairs and out into the street. He would go down and greet the flood, usher it in so that it would cleanse the town of false promises, tuberculosis and all the other incurable diseases, the worst of which was his own life without Lily. The rain itself was hard and quiet, no longer punishing the pavement but falling down into itself. There was a new sound, the distant, alluring roar of the river. All around his feet, masses of water, newborn waterfalls, instant whirlpools. A trash can freed of its mooring floated toward him. He pushed it away and watched it go tilting down the stream. His heart pounding, Tom slogged ahead, rejoicing in this water that left no path behind him, no footsteps to retrace. At the corner, he turned left to face the broad expanse of the flood. The water was deeper here. It rose from his ankles to within inches of his knees. He paused and lifted his face upward to the rain, wanting to be even wetter than he was. No amount of it would slake his thirst. For drenched as he was, his heart was still dry.

The noise of the river grew louder. He descended toward

the wooden footbridge that crossed into Watervliet. He had to see the flood from the bridge. His mother would be missing him. She would be at the bay window, holding back the lace curtains, peering into the rain for a sign. But he could not think of that. His was an act of repudiation of caution. He had tried with his kiss to stop her from dying, but it hadn't worked. This came next.

He grasped the handrail of the footbridge and made his way to the center where the bridge arched before descending to Watervliet. He stood there, gazing down into the torrent below. He could feel the heartbeat of the river thumping against the floor of the bridge. It had the same rhythm as his own! He was fully aroused, expectant, like someone wanting to make love.

The water was rising rapidly. Already the bridge throbbed and groaned under the pummeling. What if it broke? Tom had never felt so keenly alive. Every part of him relished toying with this danger, this venturing so far that he might be irretrievable. He raised his head, taking the rain in his teeth, shouting into it with whoops of joy. "I love you, Lily," he shouted, above the roar of the river. "I love you!" But he could not climb the rigging of his still-breaking voice.

I'm going to leave this place, he thought. Get out of Troy. His mother was right. It is a godforsaken hole. He gazed down. The wild current at his feet was like something let out of its cage for the first time. All at once, that portion of the railing that he held was whisked from his grasp. Tom backed away from the naked edge of the bridge. A moment later he heard a crack and a groan as the bridge bent upon itself and sank. Only the single beam to which Tom clung protruded from the flood. He felt the water hit him on the shoulder, he was in the river, in pain, holding to the beam with his good arm. The river reached out and slapped him in the face, driving water into his throat.

Coughing, gagging, Tom pulled himself higher on the beam. His lungs, already full of water, seemed to have no room for air. He struggled for breath. So this is what it is like, he thought, not being able to breathe, just holding on until you die. A powerful punch of water upon his back knocked loose the cough he needed to raise the fluid from his lungs. And he could breathe once more. Still another wallop broke his hold on the beam, and he was being carried along in the current, now submerged, now surfacing, his arms and legs strewn about him. He would not struggle. He would be like any of the helpless shapes that swept by him. He would offer himself. Besides, there wasn't any use in struggling.

In a week or so, when the flood was over, he would be found floating somewhere downstream. They would fish him out with a chain and a rope like that man Billy and he had seen. He thought of that sodden bloated corpse. And at once, his outflung hand filled with leaves. He closed it and held on, feeling himself jerked back from the current. Turning he saw that he had hold of a branch of the willow tree that was trailing in the stream. Steeling himself against the pain in his shoulder, he pulled himself hand over hand until his feet felt the solid bed of the river. He pulled himself erect, then toppled over into the shallow mud. He was out of the current. Safe.

"Why did you do it, Tom? Just tell me that, why?" It was his mother, peeling off his wet clothes. "Judas Priest! There's a bone sticking through your skin. Now see what you've done. Why? I asked you. You'd better tell me, you foolish boy."

"It's only the collarbone," said his father. "Billy, pull his shoulders back as hard as you can, like this. There, you see? That reduces the bone back inside. Hold him there while I clean it up and stitch the wound."

He watched his father's face as he rolled the warm wet plaster in a figure-of-eight around his chest, under his arm, then over and back again. Over and over until the splint was thick, molded with infinite gentleness. It had been years since he had felt his father's touch. He thought of him coming out of the whorehouse wearing his gray fedora and with a Lucky Strike hanging from his lip. A wave of affection overtook him for this gray, carbon-lipped man who all these years had faithfully sutured winter to spring, summer to fall in this cheerless town and never once berated himself for having chosen misery as the color of his life. He doesn't have long to live, thought Tom. He is dying too.

When the plaster splint had dried, the doctor spoke:

"Your mother asked you a question, Tom. Why did you do it?"

But Tom did not answer. He didn't really know why himself, only that he had to go down to the river. He needed to dare, to be valorous, for Lily and not just have her die and that's that. He had to mark her passing with some deed of his own, even his own death. He hadn't counted on the river refusing, insisting that he go back to Troy where he belonged. But he couldn't tell them any of that.

"It was that girl, wasn't it?" said his mother. "It was Lily. I knew the minute they brought her here, something awful would happen."

During the night the rain petered out and stopped. The sudden absence of the sound of its falling woke Tom up. He sat and listened to the silence that extended outward from his bed to fill the whole town. Once before he had heard such a silence when, from the landing at the head of the stairs, he could no longer hear Lily breathing.

He lay back in bed, thinking of Lily and of the sound of the river which was her sound too, murmuring, whispering, breathing, coughing, saying his name in a hundred different ways.

The next morning, the air was still, the sun came out. Almost at once the floodwaters receded from Troy. From beneath the brawling water the inert city stirred and, baffled, mute, embarrassed, began to extricate itself. One by one the doors and windows opened. People peered out, stepped into the filthy street, full of mud and stones. They called to one another, poked among the debris. Tom sat in the bay window and looked out over the city. I'm going to get out of here, he thought again. But even then he knew that flight or exile was a kind of dying. Living meant always coming back to Troy.

Like everyone else on the block, Doctor Fogarty and his wife were out on the front stoop surveying the wreckage. Here and there quiet puddles reflected the blue sky.

"I'm worried about that boy," Irene said to her husband. "He's looking pale. You don't suppose . . . ?"

The doctor scanned the sky. "There's no rainbow," he said. "The least we deserve is a rainbow."

"A rainbow over Troy would be Heaven getting sarcastic," she replied.

He smiled. The remark reminded him why he had married her.

It started snowing early in November before the Trojans had gathered themselves together to sweep up and hose down the city. The low-lying streets were still littered with branches of trees, mud and penitent stones.

When the snow fell and covered the debris, Tom's mother was relieved. She'd face up to it in the spring.

Just about then the bakery switched over to trucks. They were painted in the same old Freihofer colors—red, orange, yellow and black. They looked like toys.

"What happened to the horse?" Tom asked. "What did they do to him?"

"What horse?" said Hank. "Ooh, *that* horse," finally remembering something that had happened a long time ago. "The one that used to pull my old wagon?" Hank threw back his head, clicked his tongue twice, and turned on the ignition.

"Giddap," he hollered, and drove away.

The first week in December, Doctor Fogarty sawed through the plaster splint and took it off.

"The bone's not straight," he told Tom. "The splint didn't hold it. You're going to have a bump."

In the mirror Tom saw the mass on the left side between his neck and shoulder. It was the size of a plum, and the overlying skin was bluish red and shiny. Like a badge, it seemed to draw light to itself. He touched it with his fingertips.

"Don't fool with it," said his father. "If you let it be, maybe it'll go down some."

But as the weeks went by and the lump remained the same size, Tom knew that the deformity was permanent. Sometimes, without thinking, he would press the bony hard mass and experience a deep aching sensation which, far from causing him distress, pleased him strangely.

By Christmas, Tom no longer believed in the horse-god. Perhaps it had just been something he had made up to tell Lily, to make her laugh or keep her alive and he had talked himself into it, the way you do when you invent things.

But he would never stop believing that it was the manure, that golden vaporous Grace coming with its sweet message, that made Lily and him turn toward each other at precisely the same instant; Lily looking downward and to the right from the bay window of 104; him, down there in the street, looking upward and to the right, over his shoulder. And that it had been the manure that caused them, after the moment of surprise, to laugh, him in embarrassment, Lily with her hand covering her mouth. Sometimes, months later, when his window was open and he heard laughter or singing, he would race down the street to see a white curtain stirring in a bay window and feel the flaring of that brightness.

In the years that followed, Tom did leave Troy, but never for good. Everywhere he went, he found a strange vacancy that only this sour, unsmiling Troy did not have.

Whenever he got off the train at Sixth Avenue and Federal, he would carry his suitcase straight down to that river into which he had once plunged and which had rejected him, and out of which he had emerged purged of his childhood, wounded, and with the awful knowledge of what could happen to a man, but not why. And with the understanding that love makes grief, and grief, love. For, if anything, he loved Lily more.

And so he would return to rummage in that city of soot and Swiss-cheese lungs, leaning his ear toward echoes, looking in the luminous shadows for evidence of that summer when he had been trapped in the elaborate webs of love.

The Bee

"You cannot get lost on the Métro." This, from exile and tourist alike, each of whom has come to Paris and found his way. But they did not count on the unsurefooted, those of us born without any sense of direction. In that portion of our brains where ordinarily is housed the compass, there is a blank gray convolution. To this bland acellular place messages of *situation* shoot from eye, ear, foot. But here there is no board of synapses to connect with, or be relayed from, only a shapeless paste where information swirls and gusts until its energy is spent. Where am I? telegraphs the foot in vain. Is this east or south? implores the eye. Silence. Now this is a defect which, after fifty years of blindman's buff, is no longer irritating to me. I merely allow an extra forty minutes for any given journey—time to get lost and found. Still, it is exasperating to everyone else. What at first may be indulged as a rather lovable forgetfulness soon becomes a nettle that can fatally sting the most solid of relationships. I suppose the ideal marriage would consist of two utterly directionless people, or two with perfect homing powers. The latter, the homers, coming equipped with internal stars to steer by, deserve no compassion. Nor shall I give them any. The former, my type, would spend their lives in blissful confusion, setting forth from home armed, one with a clever little ax with which to blaze tree trunks, the other with a pouch of rice for judicious scattering. How happily this man and wife would mill about, at last presenting themselves, flowerlike, for some kind stranger to pluck and carry off to wherever it is they want to go.

One of the ways a man ought not to have to measure up is in the following of directions. What matter the ground you tread so long as you are looking at the stars? Still, in the company of another who is bent upon getting someplace on time, the affliction is apt to fulminate, proving deadly to an evening at the opera or any hope of consolation afterward. Some might think it unmanly to sit at the wheel of a car mindlessly obeying the commands issued by a woman who is incompletely resigned to her fate.

"Do you know how to get there?" you ask sweetly.

"You have been there a dozen times before." There is a hint of malice in her voice. "Just drive." And so you do, following each order as it is snapped out. "Turn right." You do. "Left at the light. Turn right here, and get into the right lane. It's the next exit." Twenty minutes and a half-dozen turns later, miraculously, you are there. But how did she know? you marvel. Once again you have been guided through a trackless desert.

Some months ago I was in Paris for the first time. I had no such navigator, and I *did* get lost on the Métro. Oft and again. I had but to descend below street level, pass through the gate to a place where two or more possibilities presented themselves and, presto! I was lost. No amount of folding and unfolding of the map of Paris or the Plan de Métro would unravel the mystery. I could only hope that the stranger I accosted would know the way and, more to the point, would deliver the directions in a French so slow and clear that even I could understand it. All too often I have tugged a French sleeve and bleated with schoolroom precision, *"Excusez-moi, monsieur, pouvez-vous m'aider?"* only to have the answer shot forth like a barrage—salvo upon salvo of words whizzing past my ears to peter out uselessly. *"Merci beaucoup,"* I must then manage, and try someone else.

One evening, having been rendered reckless by two glasses of pastis at La Coupole, I descended into the Métro at Montparnasse, blindly selected a passageway and hurried to the platform just as a train came to a halt. In the faith that I was headed for the Bastille, I threw myself aboard. Half an hour and two transfers later I dismounted to find myself in no Bastille whatsoever but in Les Pyramides. I read the sign with astonishment. Had I, once aboard the Métro, been plunged into magical sleep only to awaken in Egypt, for God's sake? The streets of Les Pyramides were dark and virtually empty. Here and there a pale face organized out of the shadows, murmured something that sounded like *m'approache* or *garçon*, and then vanished. At the end of the rue Thérèse I saw the lights and terrace of a café set into the night like a mirage. *À bas la Bastille!* I would study the map and try to find the way back to my hotel.

"You are American?" It was the young man next to me at the bar.

"Yes," I said. "You can tell? *Vous le savez?*"

He pointed to the map and shrugged. "I make a guess." It was a moment before I recognized his words as English. Heavily accented, but English. Now after three weeks of struggling with French in Provence and three days of a silence in Paris such as to suppose that the God Harpocrates with finger at lips had shushed me, I was thrilled, as much by my own voice as his. No sound in recent memory had so satisfied my ear. Lost in the darkling Pyramids, engulfed in a sandstorm of French grammar, I could have wept for joy.

"May I buy you a pastis?" He accepted with silent grace.

"I am Greek," he said. "My name is Ari. You know, the same as Onassis." Ari looked about thirty-five. In fact, he was twenty-six as I saw on the passport he showed me with pride. Large swarthy men often do look older than they are.

"I weigh one hundred ninety-five pounds," he said as though declaring his body to a customs official. I felt it only fair to tell him that I was fifty-three years old and weighed one hundred thirty pounds. Nothing so cements a chance meeting of foreigners in an alien land as the exchange of vital statistics. It was a good way to begin.

"I am merchant seaman," he said. "On my third voyage I jump ship in Boston. I live there four and a half years. Boston is beautiful. I lose my mind." Together we remember The Commons, Beacon Hill, the Charles River and Faneuil Hall.

"It is churlish of me to be in Paris for the first time," I said, "and to feel nostalgic for Boston."

"What is *churlish*?" he asked. "What is *nostalgic*?"

"Ungrateful. Homesick. What brought you to Paris?"

"The immigration officers pick me up one day. I am in Greenwich Village then. Greenwich Village—I lose my mind! They catch me in the street. This is it. The next day—out. But I will go back," said Ari grimly. "One day I will live in the States." He paused and leaned closer. "I have a plan. I look for a ship that goes to Mexico. When I get to Mexico I take a walk—across the border into your country. Then I get married with an American girl. I pay her four thousand dollars. In one year I get a divorce. Then I can stay. It is simple."

"Umm," I said. "It doesn't sound too good to me. Don't

THE BEE

you need to have identification to get a marriage license?"

Ari was miffed. "*Pas difficile.* Nobody checks up. That is the way it is done. Don't worry about it." I ordered more pastis.

"What is your work?" he asked. "Are you a professor?"

"I am a doctor. But not this month. This month I am a writer. I have been in Provence for three weeks trying to write."

"What kind of doctor?"

"A surgeon."

"You cut people open?" He gripped his belly in exaggerated horror. There were two Band-Aids on the knuckles of his hand. The dressings were filthy. Through each, a dark stain had penetrated and dried.

"How did you hurt yourself?"

The smile broadened. "In France you are not a doctor. You told me so yourself." But he peeled off the Band-Aids and showed me the scabs underneath.

"Almost healed," I announced.

"Yes, almost." He wadded up the Band-Aids and dropped them into an ashtray, then made and unmade his fist as though to limber it up. The skin that had been covered with adhesive was white and clean next to the rest.

"You will like to take a walk with me?" He asked this shyly, afraid that I might decline. We left the bar. Several turns later I was, of course, irretrievably lost. As is my custom, I surrendered to expertise.

"Where are we going?"

"To Montmartre. You will see life there. You will lose your mind."

"It is my body that I usually lose," I told him. "I never know quite where I am. It drives my wife crazy. I must always be led about. Like Samson."

"Then I shall be the boy who leads you by the hand," he said. The idea suddenly amused him. He laughed loudly

201

and without restraint. He stopped, and then again the laughter came, propagating itself, infecting me. At last he was through. He wiped his eyes.

"You are a great man. You make me laugh. I never laugh so much since I come to Paris. You make me feel happy. I forget my troubles. I love America."

The streets grew busier. Crowds of people, cars, street musicians, cafés spilling onto the sidewalks. I heard languages other than French—German, Spanish, Japanese. Behind a man and woman Ari slowed almost to a standstill, his ear cocked.

"They are speaking Greek," he said with a smile. "Beautiful Greek."

"Does it make you homesick to hear it?"

He shrugged. We spoke then of the Greek Islands—Évvoia, where one of my sons was spending the summer, and Mykonos, Ari's favorite because of the nude beaches. I thought of what he had given up. The Greek sun, the blue Aegean, in exchange for the hallucinations of Paris nights; the poppies and lizards of Mykonos for the fat bowlegged little French dogs that squat to defecate in the streets.

An October wind had come up. Ari pulled the collar of his jacket about his neck. He walked with a loose gait, planting his feet widely. The pavement might have been a deck where he must allow for the swelling of the sea. Again and again our shoulders would touch, stick to each other, hold for a moment, then part. We stopped to listen to a young woman playing the mandolin on the street. In front of her lay the open case of her instrument. She had long red hair, blue eyes and the pale freckled skin of so many girls in Boston. The expression on her face was dreamy, distracted.

"She is Irish," said Ari. "She has been playing on the streets for five years."

"Do you know her?"

"Yes." He nodded, then walked up behind the girl, cupped her shoulders lightly with his hands and bent to whisper something in her ear. She gave no sign of having heard but remained absorbed in the thin sound she was making with her fingers. Still, he and the girl seemed at that moment to share a condition of which I could not partake.

"She is . . . *déboussole*," he said when he returned to my side. "Coo-coo. You know . . . the compass is lost."

"What did you say to her?"

"I told her to go back to Ireland before it is too late." I dug into my pocket and dropped a handful of coins into the mandolin case. Again, she made no sign of having noticed. We walked on.

"And you?" I asked. "Why don't you go home?" But it was no use. He had abruptly canceled Greece.

"How much did you give her?"

"I don't know. A few francs."

"She does well enough."

"I need to find a W.C.," I told him.

"Ah. You need to piss. Wait a moment." He led the way into a side street lined with parked cars. He pointed between two of the cars.

"Piss here," he said, and noting my hesitation, he stepped to the corner of the block where he waited discreetly.

Ari quickened his pace. I doubled my steps to keep up. The yellow leaves of the chestnut trees stuck to our shoes before screeching off in search of refuge.

"What do you like to do?" he asked. "Do you like the sea?"

"God, no. Only rowing gently on a river, and not against the current either."

He laughed. "You are lazy."

"No. Old. Yes. Lazy. But I do like to climb trees without

being watched, then sit in the branches for a long time. And you? What do you like?" A phalanx of hilarious students came along, broke apart upon us, then rejoined behind.

"What do you want?" I repeated.

"When? Now?" His smile was wary.

"No, in life. Your goal, what is it?"

"I told you before. I have only one goal. To live in America."

"Where do you live now?"

"A bad place. It is dirty. Every day they take from me eighty francs. Last night I wake up . . . and there is a mouse on my arm."

We turned into a smaller, darker side street, then another. One more turn took us into what was little more than an alley. There was no one there. A single streetlamp at the corner gave a soiled gray light. The tiny window balconies of the buildings on either side of the alley bent close to each other almost touching. Ari stopped and leaned against the wall of a building.

"Where do you like to go now?" he asked. I looked at my watch. Eleven-thirty. We had been together for more than two hours.

"It's getting late." I said. "I think I had better go back to my hotel in Montparnasse if you will tell me how to get there. This has been the best evening I have spent in France."

Ari was silent. As I watched, the perpetual smile slid from his face and was replaced by a congealed grin. It was as though his jaw had become dislocated. He leaned back against the wall, one knee bent so that the sole of that foot was flat against the building. There was the suggestion of immense strength and agility. I had the feeling that he was capable of hurtling from that position and sprinting away. Or in pursuit. He was like a motor idling. His eyes! Had I really looked into them before? They slid from side to side, pausing for only a fraction of a second at the midpoint of his vision, where I stood. It appeared that he was weighing some action. It seemed to me that he was on the verge of saying something, yet unable to say it, in possession of a secret that he was tempted to tell, but must not. The silence between us lengthened.

"What's on your mind?" I asked at last. "What are you thinking about?" He did not answer, but continued, I thought, to suffer the containment of something.

"Look, Ari, if you want to tell me something, say it, for heaven's sake." But already, I was not sure that I wanted to hear. Quietly then, without emphasis, he spoke.

"I am a prostitute," he said. The rolled *r* gave the word a mysterious and palpable thrill. A shudder caressed my belly. "You give me two hundred francs and I spend the night with you." I felt the skin of my face tighten with shock.

"No," I said at last. "I am truly sorry. It is a misunderstanding. I must go home now."

"But you do not know the way."

"Never mind. I'll find it."

"Two hundred francs is too much for you? I will take one hundred fifty. I like you very much." His offer was quick, like those of the Arab boys who sell leather briefcases on the street and who dog the tracks of tourists, lowering the price with each step.

"You don't like me? I think you like me too much. Believe me, you will lose your mind. How much *will* you pay me?"

"I am sorry to have used up your time." I reached for his hand, took it in mine, and released it. "I shall always remember this evening. You have been very kind and generous."

The body tautened. Through his shirt, I saw that the rise and fall of respiration had ceased. He was coiled to spring. I turned then and walked away. I was trembling, the pulse battering at my ribs. Would he follow? Come in a rush from behind? Had I not seen the calligraphy of violence just beneath the skin of his face? Had I not a moment before held one of those strangler's hands in mine? There! Just at his belt a gleam toward which one of his hands twitched. I glanced about for a witness. Someone who would hear the faint hiss of unsheathing, see the lightning raised in his fist, the pumping of that mighty forearm, and who would report these things to . . . to whom? Some official who would listen and cover a yawn with his hand. I must not run, I thought. And forced myself to walk slowly. Four steps. Eight. Fifteen. Counting. Twenty. Then turned to see. I had to. He stood where I had left him, tilted against the wall, off kilter to the rest of the city. Nor did he look after me, but sagged there, his gaze absorbed in the pavement at his feet. All at once he threw back his head and coughed hugely. A thread of blood appeared on his chin. He shook his head. His thumb and fingertips were at his eyes, holding down the lids. He no longer appeared burly, rapacious, only pale and sick. Exhausted, a god weary from having no worshippers. I thought of the inherent decency of the man that had made him hesitate to announce himself. I knew, too, that for a couple of hours it was he who had lost his mind.

I made my way back to the hotel. For the first time I did not get lost. The room was white and ascetic as a monk's cell. I felt unwell, fell across the desolate bed, shivering. With what? The dreadful weight of monotony. Again and again, the same thoughts. It was his own fault. He should not have waited so long to declare himself. And now it was too late. He would not be able to find someone else. It would be a night lost. I thought of the eighty francs he needed every day for that verminous room. Why had I not given him the money? What kept me from it? It was terror, I knew, that blinded me. But even then, even as I walked away from him, struggling to keep from looking back, even then, more than anything else, I had wanted to see his knife, wanted even to ask him: Let me see your knife. I closed my eyes and saw again the soft pressure of his lips around the dead butt of a cigarette that he did not bother to dislodge, his hair upgathered at the back of his neck like Apollo's. But what other god could he have been? Perhaps the sorrow is all mine, I thought. Perhaps he has come to accept himself as he is. There would be no ship to Mexico, no *mariage blanc*. He is addicted to his fate. He would not have it otherwise. Yet, so impatient for reincarnation in a better land. All his dark voyaging . . . like a lunatic laboring to step into his mirage.

It was the noise of revelers that ushered back my life. Outside my window a band of students on the way to La Coupole was singing. Huddled above exuberance, I felt old, used up. I thought of Ari submerged in Paris like a pincered thing. As though I had fallen overboard and sunk to the bottom only long enough for one lungful of air to last, then shot to the surface, gasping, wondering whether he would have attacked had I stayed a moment longer. Or had he simply let me go in a moment of despair or, worse, of an affection for which he would reproach himself?

It was the next day. Outside my window Paris went on being Paris. I rose, showered and left the hotel, walking, as was my custom, from Montparnasse to the Jardin du Luxembourg. On the way I stopped, as I did each day, at a small patisserie. Inside, singly and in clusters, dozens of coppery bees were feeding on the fruit tarts. Their delicate buzz was an echo, but an echo only, of the bee-charged vineyards of Provence that I had left the week before. Provence, with the calm grapes ripening among the turbulence.

"Tarte au citron," I said, and pointed. A woman brushed bees away gently and wrapped the tart in a square of pink tissue paper, twisting the ends to seal it. But she had not seen what I saw! One bee, camouflaged by an edge of burnt meringue, vibrated on, its wings trapped in the sticky stuff. I continued on to the park with its statues and benches and precise flowerbeds. My heart was pounding. By a bed of dahlias and tiger lilies I knelt and unwrapped the tart.

"Bee," I said aloud. "I want neither your honey nor your sting." With a fingernail I disimpacted the prisoner and waved it up and away. Then, protected from myself by the flowers, I ate. It was the most delicious tart of my life. I should never taste its like again. The lemon rind bitter as the lips of a sailor in a tempest, the meringue sweet as the milk of bees.

It is weeks later, and I have recaptured the pace of my life. Yesterday a packet of photographs arrived. There is one of myself taken by a helpful stranger in the Luxembourg Garden. What I see is a shabby middle-aged man, stooped and in need of a haircut. He wears wrinkled, mismatched clothing, like someone who has been traveling too long. Now, each day I patrol the corridors of the hospital where I work, then stand at the operating table. A young surgeon stands opposite me.

"Hold the scalpel this way," I say to him. And I take his hand in mine to guide him. In the touching of our hands, in our two voices mingling, the old covenant is forged again. The wisdom of the craft is being passed on. But now and then I also hear the voice and feel the hand of another who shapes and colors these words, and who looms above my thoughts. Where had those hands been?

I wondered. What done? That tongue? Who am I? I ask myself. And answer: He that remembers.

I remember his hesitation to speak, a balance of caution and recklessness. Ah, but he is not evil, only doomed, perhaps, to atone for the evil of others. A latter-day pagan transforming Paris into Alexandria, scouting the darkest alleys, perishable and more beautiful than the Fountain of the Medicis, lither than the Seine, offering his occult choice pleasures in the shadow of Notre Dame, that deadweight pile of piety where the only passion is that of candles dying in their trays. I cannot imagine him in the daylight. Did he, each morning, promise to start a new life? But then would come night, black and glittering, tempting him out of his room, away from the mice and the monotony to the palpitating pavement of Paris? Look! He returns to me as a bolo returns to the hand that has hurled it away. There is his face, like the moon, with the purple night inflaming his hair, leaning against that wall, idling, his flesh charged with a whole Niagara of ardor. Then shipwrecked.

It is evening. My wife and I are in the car driving to the theater.

"Which way do I go?" I ask her.

"You tell me," she says.

"I have told what I can," I say. "The rest I shall tell to those I meet in Hell."

"What in the world are you talking about?" she says. "Turn right at the corner."

My Brother Shaman

In the cult of the Bhagavati, as it has been practiced in southern India, there is a ritual in which two entranced shamans dressed in feathered costumes and massive headgear enter a circle of witnesses. All night long in the courtyard of a temple they lunge and thrust at each other, give shouts of defiance, make challenging gestures. It is all done to the sound of drums, conches and horns. Come daybreak, the goddess Kali "slays" the demon Darika, then plunges her hands into the very bowels of Darika, drinking of and smearing herself with blood. At last Kali withdraws from the field of battle having adorned herself with the intestines of the vanquished.

It is a far cry from the bloody trances of shamans to the bloody acts of surgery. Or is it? Take away from Kali and Darika the disciplinary beat of tautened hide and the moaning of flutes, and you have . . . an emergency intestinal resection. The technique is there, the bravado, the zeal. Only lacking in surgery is the ecstasy.

In both surgery and shamanism the business is done largely by the hands of the operator. The surgeon holds his scalpel, hemostat, forceps; the shaman, his amulet of bone, wood, metal. For each there is the hieratic honoring of ritual objects. The handling of these objects induces a feeling of tranquillity and power. One's mind is nudged from the path of self-awareness into the pathless glade of the imagination. The nun, too, knows this. She tells her beads, and her heart is enkindled. Surely it is true that the handling of instruments is conducive to the kind of possession or devotion that is the mark of all three—nun, surgeon, shaman. The surgeon and the shaman understand that one must honor, revere and entreat one's tools. Both do their handiwork with a controlled vehemence most dramatically seen in those offshoots of Buddhism wherein the shaman ties his fingers in "knots," giving them a strange distorted appearance. These priests have an uncanny flexibility of their finger joints, each of which has a special name. During these maneuvers the shaman is possessed by finger spirits. He invokes the good spirits and repels the evil ones. Such hand poses, or mudras, seen in Buddhist iconography, are used in trancelike rituals to call down the gods to possess the shaman. In like manner the surgeon restrains his knife even as he gives it rein. He, too, is the medium between man and God.

The shaman has his drum which is the river of sound through which he can descend to the Kingdom of Shadows to retrieve the soul of his tribesfellow. The surgeon listens to the electronic beep of the cardiac monitor, the regulated respiration of anesthesia, and he is comforted or warned. Even the operating table has somewhat the shape and size of the pagan altars I saw in a tiny sixth-century baptistry in the Provençal village of Vénasque. Upon these slabs beasts and, in certain instances, humans were laid open to appease the gods. Should one of these ancient pagans undergo resurrection and be brought to a modern operating room with its blazing lamps and opulence of linen and gleaming gadgetry, where masked and gowned figures dip their hands in and out of the body of someone who has been plunged into magical sleep, what else would he think but that he had happened upon a ritual sacrifice?

Nor is the toilet of decoration less elaborate for surgeon than for shaman. Take the Washing of the Hands: Behold the surgeon at his ablutions. His lavabo is a deep sink, often of white porcelain, with a central faucet controlled by the knee. The soap he uses is thick and red as iodine. It is held in a nozzled bottle on the wall. The surgeon depresses a pedal on the floor. Once, twice, three times and collects in his cupped palm a puddle of the soap. There it would sit, lifeless, if he did not add a little water from the faucet and begin to brush. Self-containment is part of the nature of soap. Now, all at once, suds break as air and water are incorporated. Here and there in the play of the bristles, bubbles, first one, then another and another, lift from the froth and achieve levitation. For a moment each globule sways in front of the surgeon's dazzled eyes, but only long enough to give him its blessing before winking out. Meanwhile, the stern brush travels back and forth through the slush of forearms, raising wakes of gauze, scratching the skin . . . Oh, not to hurt or abrade, but tenderly, as one scratches the ears of a dog. At last the surgeon thrusts his hands into the stream of water. A dusky foam darkens the porcelain and fades like smoke. A moment later the sink is calm and white. The surgeon too is calm. And purified.

The washing of the hands, then, is at once a rational step in the achievement of sterile technique and a ritual act carried out under the glance of God by which one is made ready to behold, to perform. It is not wholly unlike the whirling of dervishes, or the to and fro rocking of the orthodox Jew at his prayers. The mask, cap, gown and gloves that the surgeon puts on prior to surgery echo, do they not, the phylacteries of this same Jew? Prophetic wisdom, if it will come at all, is most likely to come to one so sacredly trussed. By these simple acts of bathing and adorning, both surgeon and shaman are made receptacular.

Time was when, in order to become a shaman, one had to undergo an initiatory death and resurrection. The aspirant had to be taken to the sky or the netherworld; often he would be dismembered by spirits, cooked in a pot and eaten by them. Only then could he be born again as a shaman. No such rite of passage goes into the making of a surgeon, it is true, but there is something about the process of surgical training that is reminiscent of the sacred ur-drama after all. The modern surgical intern must undergo a long and arduous novitiate during which the subjugation of the will and spirit to the craft is virtually complete. After a number of years of abasement and humiliation he or she is led to a room where no one else is permitted. There is the donning of special raiment, the washing of the hands and, at last, the performance of secret rites before the open ark of the body. In this, surgery remains a hieratic pantomime marked by exorcism, propitiation and invocation. God dwells in operating rooms as He does everywhere. More than once I have surmised a presence . . . something between hearing and feeling. . . .

In the selection of students to enter medical school, I wonder whether the present weight given to academic excellence in organic chemistry is justified. At least as valid a selection would be based upon the presence of a bat-shaped mole on the inner aspect of the thigh of the aspirant, or a specific conjunction of the planets on his birthday. Neither seems more prophetic than the other in the matter of intuition, compassion and ingenuity which form the trinity of doctorhood.

The shaman's journey through disorder and illness to health has parallels to the surgeon's journey into the body. Both are like Jason setting out in the Argos, weathering many storms to return at last with the Golden Fleece. Or Galahad with the Holy Grail. The extirpated gallbladder, then, becomes the talisman of the surgeon's journey, the symbol of his hard-won manhood. What is different is that the surgeon practices inherited rites, while the shaman is susceptible to visions. Still, they both perform acts bent upon making chaos into cosmos.

Saint John of the Cross alludes to the mystic as a solitary bird who must seek the heights, admit of no companionship even with its own kind, stretch out its beak into the air, and sing sweetly. I think of such a shaman soaring, plummeting, riding ecstatic thermals to the stars, tumbling head over heels, and at last descending among the fog of dreams. If, as it seems, the mark of the shaman was his ability to take flight, soaring to the sky or plummeting to the earth in search of his quarry, only the astronaut or the poet would now qualify.

Ever since Nietzsche delivered his stunning pronouncement—"Dead are all the gods"—man has been forced to assume the burden of heroism without divine assistance. All the connections to the ancestral past have been severed. It is our rashest act. For no good can come to a race that refuses to acknowledge the living spirit of ancient kingdoms. Ritual has receded from the act of surgery. Only the flavor of it is left, giving, if not to the performers, then to the patients and to those forbidden to witness these events, a shiver of mysticism. Few and far between are the surgeons who consider what they do an encounter with the unknown. When all is said and done, I am left with the suspicion that we have gone too far in our arrogant drift from the priestly forebears of surgery. It is pleasing to imagine surgeons bending over their incisions with love, infusing them with the impalpable. Only then would the surgeon, like the shaman, turn himself into a small god and re-create the world.

Taking the World In for Repairs

INTERPLAST. It stands for International Plastic Surgeons, Incorporated. The organization was conceived in 1969 by Donald Laub to bring plastic and reconstructive surgery to indigent people of the Third World, to train the native surgeons in operative techniques and to forge professional relationships that would endure, would outlast any political differences between countries. Twenty-five years ago I was chief resident in surgery at Yale. Don was one of my interns. Now he practices plastic surgery in Palo Alto, California. Since it began, INTERPLAST has performed more than ten thousand operations on many dozens of expeditions to those parts of the world termed "undeveloped"—Mexico, Honduras, Ecuador, the Philippines, Jamaica and Peru. Sometimes a single person is sent out; sometimes, a team of twenty. All are volunteers. The length of this expedition to Peru will be two weeks. The doctors, nurses and technicians will come from five universities—Yale, Stanford, Johns Hopkins, Emory and the University of West Virginia—and from seven of the United States—Nevada, Kentucky, California, Connecticut, Georgia, West Virginia and Maryland.

• • •

The trip from North to South America is hardly Xenophon's march from Babylon to the Bosporus; still, it is in the heroic mold. Twenty people, all unused to and resisting regimentation, each with that certain "sweet arrogance" that belongs to men and women trained to a fare-thee-well in their life's work—it is not easy. In Miami, a surgeon wanders away; in Lima, a nurse stops listening and misses a vital connection. Yet in the end we have been coaxed and prodded on and off the succession of planes, buses and cars that have carried us to Peru. Seventy crates and cartons of equipment have been ushered through customs. INTERPLAST uses none of the precious resources of the host country. We have brought our own—sterile gauze, hemostats, scalpels, all.

We are assembled in the lobby of the Hotel Crillon in Lima. The next morning we fly to Arequipa in the southern highlands. We shall work there in a government provincial hospital named Honorio Delgado. In the evening an exuberance possesses us, a kind of glee at the prospect of shared labor and adventure. Friendships which had been initiated in airports along the way are cemented. Absent is the wariness of new acquaintances inching toward intimacy. There is no taking of measure, no hesitation. The team is being forged. A MASH mentality prevails. Veterans of previous expeditions regale novices with tales of surgical derring-do. The initiates sigh and fidget. Later I fall asleep dreaming of Peru. Of condors and gold, of llamas and emerald mountains, of cruel Pizzaro and his conquistadores.

The flight from Lima to the mountain city of Arequipa takes little more than an hour, but I think the direction must be straight up. Soon we are flying among the white peaks. What a harsh rudimentary land! It is at once epic

216

and mysterious. Even the sky seems studded with hiero-glyphs. Abruptly, Peru vanishes and we are engulfed in fog. Peaks and crags dodge our wings and miss, but barely. The plane flutters, banks, rolls all but over, and we are on the ground. It is less a descent and landing than a careful insertion into Arequipa. Half of us are to be housed in Peruvian homes, the rest are wedged, three to a tiny room, at Turistas, a pink and green hotel made of volcanic rock. We do not stop to unpack but rush to the hospital to begin our work. The great clinic we are told, is already in session. CONSULTORIO CHIRUGIA PLÁSTICA DE INTERPLAST reads the sign on the wall. Black crayon on yellow paper. Within minutes we are fully engaged in the examination and se-lection of patients for the days of surgery ahead.

The hospital of Honorio Delgado is slowly, impercep-tibly settling into a state of splendid ruination. One day it will be the twentieth century's medical Machu Picchu. The floor bears great gouges where tile and stone have crum-bled. The ceiling is a constellation of cracks. Should some-thing break, it stays broken. There is no such thing as restoration or replacement. Again and again Honorio Del-gado has run out of catgut, scrub suits, dressings. Rubber gloves are mended and reused the next day and the day after that. Each scrap of gauze is retrieved from a bucket, washed and folded and made ready to blot another pa-tient's blood. The scalpels of Arequipa enjoy longevity. If these knives could speak, they would each spin tales of their dozens of incisions. At Yale or Stanford, a knife has a lifetime of a single operation. Each procedure here is dictated by the cost of the material needed to do it. The staff is paid, but poorly. Before an emergency appendec-tomy, the patient must buy the suture material, gauze and knife blade to be used upon him. If there is no money, as is usual, the residents themselves must buy the material, paying for the right to heal their patients. While INTER-

PLAST, ah INTERPLAST, has come to Peru, its cartons bursting with throwaway knives, suture material of every caliber and variety—catgut, nylon, vicryl, silk; and tanks of anesthetic gas, intravenous fluids and an array of clever instruments—dermatomes, staples, retractors, endotracheal tubes. We are both proud of and embarrassed by our plenty. Under the awed gazes of our hosts we squirm. Always, we are the rich gringos.

Clinic is held in two tiny examining rooms in which there are never fewer than a dozen people. Four examinations are being conducted simultaneously. In one corner Iris Figueroa, a beautiful fourteen-year-old girl, glows among our white coats. Her mother holds up the girl's right hand for us to see. It has but one finger, the index, which protrudes like a talon. The rest are absent save for a cluster of soft nubbins bunched at the knuckles.

Leo is our hand surgeon. "What is your name?" he asks her.

"Iris," she says and lowers her gaze.

"Wiggle your thumb," says Leo. His English is translated into Spanish by a nurse. But what can he mean? There is no thumb. He means only to see if she moves the bone at the base of what should have been her thumb, the one hidden in the featureless pad of tissue in which all five metacarpals exist uselessly. Iris tries to wiggle it; she tries very hard to do what the doctor has asked her to, even shakes her head at the effort. There is no movement to be seen. Still, palpating, Leo feels *something* at work within that pad of flesh.

"We can separate this ray out," he thinks aloud. "Make a web space, deepen it all the way to the wrist. Then she will be able to pinch." The girl's mother lifts Iris's other hand and we see that this one too is blank, blind, dumb. And fingerless. For a moment we are still. Then:

218

"Is she right- or left-handed?" The interpreter is busy.

"Right," she says at last. And we smile as though we have just received the best news. And we have. All this while, the girl has been eating our faces with her eyes.

"Put her on the schedule," says Leo. "I'll do her tomorrow."

"There's no more room on the schedule tomorrow," says Fran. She has charge of making out the operative list. "In fact, you're all booked up for the whole two weeks." Leo says nothing, only looks down at the small unfinished hand, paw really, that he still holds in his own.

"It's just the way it is," says Fran. "We can't do them all."

"You tell her, then," says Leo. There is a short volley of Spanish. Something pale and vague flits from the face of the girl. I think it must be hope. Her head drops down and away. She is trying not to show what is churning inside. But courage has its limits, in Peru as everywhere else, and there are tears. With her single finger she reaches up to wipe them away.

"No room?" Leo asks again. He cannot seem to understand.

"No room," says Fran.

"Give her a high priority slip for next year. We'll be back next year," he says to Iris. "I'll fix it then." Fran writes out a slip of paper, marks it "priority" and hands it to the mother of the girl.

Paper is shuffled, the door is let open a bit, and a woman leads a seven-year-old boy into the room. He climbs upon the table that Iris has just left. Where his lip should be is a nude rubbery insect from which a single tooth projects.

"What's your name?" asks Don. In California, he is famous for his large series of sex-change operations.

"Miguel."

Don laughs as though the name itself were funny. "Say

'*el gato,*' Miguel," he says. "Say 'Coca-Cola.' " The boy looks at his mother. She nods.

"*El gato,*" says Miguel. "Coca-Cola." But it is only an approximation. The vowels leak out of his nose; the consonants are blunted, furry.

"Unilateral cleft lip and cleft palate," says Don. "We ought to get it fixed now. Later, there will be less chance for speech improvement. He's at the right age."

"Now," says Fran. "You know there's no space for it. Why do you make me say it again and again?" She tells the mother it cannot be done, tells her to bring him back next year. She gives her a slip of paper. They rise to leave.

"Good-bye, Miguelito," said Don. "*Adiós, amigo.*" It is the boy's turn to smile.

Just at noon the sun comes out for the first time. In its rays the hospital of Honorio Delgado blanches. Through the tiny window of the examining room we turn to see the huge snowy cone of Misti, one of the three volcanoes that ring the city of Arequipa. It is dead, they say, burnt out. But I don't know about that. There is just the whiff of temper in that bit of cloud the peak has snagged. With volcanoes as with people, I suspect eruptions are a matter of anger or spite. If the gift of prophecy has not deserted me, we can expect a rush of hot lava when the "No!" index in this clinic reaches a critical point. What mountain could hold its peace in the face of so much heartbreak? Once, I arrived in Paris some hours later than I had planned only to find that the hotel had given away my room reservation. "*Complet,*" announced the desk clerk, dismissing me with her back. Very Parisian, I was to learn, after dragging my reluctant luggage into a dozen other lobbies in search of shelter only to be met each time with another "*Complet.*" It is a small thing to sit up all night in a foreign city waiting for the dawn. I know that. "No room" in Peru is worse than *"complet"* in Paris. Still, as I watch the disappointed children leave the clinic, I think of that cold and tired night.

"Look at this, will you?" says Aida, one of the nurses. She is registering the patients, carrying out triage.

"Look at what?" I say. And see the balled-up hand of the young man. Fifteen years ago he had grabbed something hot, something which stuck to his palm. When the burn had healed, his fist was permanently clenched.

Mano embalito it is called here.

"Needs excision of the cicatrix and full-thickness skin graft. Or a pedicle."

I look over at Fran. "Don't," I say. Later Fran will admit that it took her four years and six expeditions to be able to say no without crying. Fran is a specialist in international medicine. She is pretty and petite. She is fluent in Spanish. She gets things done.

The door opens. Three young women enter. They are sisters, each with the fused fingers of syndactyly on their left hands. Once again, Fran wrings out the operative schedule and a single operating space is found.

"You must decide," she says to the sisters. They whisper to themselves for a moment, then two point to the third.

"Why that one?" I want to know.

"She is getting married. Without the operation, she cannot wear her wedding ring."

I step out into the waiting room from which the throng spills to the out-of-doors where there is a topiary garden —shrubs in the shape of a llama, a condor, an ocelot, an angel, each one carved precisely as if by a surgeon of INTERPLAST. From this garden I spy on the patients. How beautiful they are. Tiny. Even the tallest of them is shorter than the least of us. Every shade of brown and gold is represented in their skin. Their hair is full and black. All their sexuality seems to reside in their hair. Again and again the children are scooped up and pressed into their mothers. The children eye each other's deformities with quiet solemnity. The mothers too cast quick glances. It is said that the Incas were all exterminated during the Spanish conquest, that their race is extinct. But I don't believe it. The genes of the Incas are here in this courtyard full of *serranos*. Now and then I see a perfect pre-Columbian face, and then I am sure.

Here, in this waiting room, one would think deformity the natural state of mankind. No child but with his cleft lip, burn scar, webbed hand. The marred and the scarred far outnumber the others. The children are quiet, reserved. There is no restlessness in them. Only, they wait. The longing in their faces is all for a clever scalpel, a tiny row of meticulously placed sutures that will redeem their lives. See how the examining room opens again. Something billows forth from the crowd. Yet no one moves. It is only their breath that has surged. The lucky name is called out: "Fabian Platera Choquehuanca." A woman carries a fully swathed infant into the examining room. The rest inhale, exhale and settle back into waiting. Many have come on foot from great distances, from villages high in the Andes. Still, they are not disgruntled. Nor are there predatory lawyers circling at the periphery. There is only the eternal eloquence of the wound. All at once, from the examining room, another "no room" followed by a hush in which I think I hear the volcano rumbling. I go back to duty. The door bangs open and a young boy of eight runs in and hugs Fran. They cling to each other, laughing. There is a barrage of Spanish. Fran explains:

"He had a double cleft lip. We fixed it last year. He and his mother have come all the way from Puno to show us. Look. You can't even tell." She turns to the boy.

"You are handsome," she says. He laughs and races out of the room.

It is a long walk from Turistas to the hospital. At eye level, the swarm and buzz of Calle Jerusalén. Glance upward and there, pale with snow and cloud, the great Andean ghosts—Misti, Chachani, Pichu Pichu. Somber and outsize, they are inert in a way that the Alps or the Rockies never are. And how much older they seem. Arequipa is white, every building made of the gleaming lava stone called *sillar*. It is porous, with many natural gouges. Plastered and whitewashed, it makes an irresistible writing surface for the slogan-crazed Peruvians. Straight through the center of the city charges the river Chili, from a distance a veritable whitewater shaking its mane over the banks. Come closer, and it is brown, feculent, stinking. Upon its banks, you stay mum. You had better. A single drop of spray upon your lip would lay you mad and frothing.

Another day. Another ten cleft lips and palates. We are pushing to get them all done, all that we have promised before we leave. Among the Indians it is believed that a congenitally deformed child is a reproof to the mother for excessive passion or aberrant desire, whatever they are. If this were so, these legions of lips and palates would accuse all of Peru.

A short lesson in embryology: Mesenchyme is that all-purpose undifferentiated tissue of which we are largely comprised early in fetal life. Mesenchyme is not stationary, but flows, folding upon itself, rising into ridges, incorporating within itself little sacs and hollows. Within the first trimester of pregnancy it happens sometimes, far oftener in Peru than in America, it seems, that the mesenchyme destined to form the upper jaw, the lip and the palate fails either to fuse in the midline of the face, or even to migrate to the midline of the face. And so there is a cleft where there should have been an uninterrupted smooth and attractive joining. Such an intrauterine mishap runs in families. Should a mother or a sibling have a cleft lip, then the odds turn grimmer for the unborn. Inbreeding, it is said, plays a part, the grouping and concentration of negative influences. And malnutrition. And multiparity in which an eleventh or twelfth child is born to a woman in her forties or later. The Indians of Peru live in just such a state of genetic vulnerability. INTERPLAST has come here to repair and reconstruct, to correct the inborn errors to which society and culture have made these people susceptible. So we tell ourselves and others. So we believe. But that is not the only reason we have come. Honesty insists that each of us is here for our own entirely other reasons. The surgical residents have come for the experience of operating on great numbers of these deformities. Within two weeks they will have performed more of these operations than most surgeons will do in a lifetime. For some, it is the opportunity for virtue that we are seeking. Such opportunities are not without the element of self-aggrandizement. For still others it is the exhilaration of the exotic that beckons, or the lovely sense of camaraderie that is to be found in working together for a purpose we think high. Last, there is the need for human beings to challenge themselves. In surgery it is best done by tackling the most difficult of clinical situations and prevailing. Next to the control of the birth rate, the correction of malnutrition, genetic counseling and the teaching of simple hygiene, all our surgery is nothing. Still, that we have come to do it is enough for us.

In the great central hall as in the courtyards outside the hospital, endless lines of Indians, many exhausted and malnourished, wait for a turn at the *farmacia*, the *sala de radiografía*. There is almost no noise, no movement. Only now and then a small enigmatic cry, a whisper, a cough. The faces of the people are patient, blank. A visit here takes an entire day, at the end of which half will not have been seen and must return the next day. The *sala de operaciones* is on the fourth floor. One climbs, of course. From the head of the stairwell to the doors of the operating theater, the corridor is jammed with the relatives of those inside and undergoing surgery. Some member of the family will remain with the patient throughout his hospital stay. Food will be brought in and fed to the patient.

Now that the days of our great clinics are over, physical examinations take place in every nook and cranny of the hospital—in the middle of a hallway, on the stairs. Indians arrive at any time, unannounced, and ask to be seen. No one is turned away by INTERPLAST. Most are given slips to return the next year. One or two lucky ones are taken then and there into the operating room and added to the day's schedule. Somehow, a woman with a paralyzed arm has made her way through the operating-room doors and into the surgeons' dressing room. She stands against a row of metal lockers hoping to be examined. Nearby a Peruvian doctor is undressing for his work. I ask the woman to remove her shirt. It is a long-sleeved pullover which she cannot manage unassisted. I help her. Now she is naked from the waist up. One year ago, she tells me, a surgeon in Cuzco removed a tumor from her armpit. Ever since, her arm has been dead. She cannot care for her children. Now the woman and the Peruvian surgeon are equally naked, each taking no notice of the other. A brachial plexus injury, I think. From the surgery. There is nothing to be done. I help her to put on the shirt.

In the operating room the ancient pedagogy of surgery goes on, but here as in Babel. The doctors and nurses of Arequipa speak no English; we, no Spanish. Still, hand guides hand within a sleeping patient. Voices murmur.

"Paciencia, paciencia. Despacio, por favor." And after a difficult technique newly mastered: *"Felicitaciones, amigo."*

As usual, the surgeons are confident; the anesthesiologists nervous. It is the role of the anesthesiologist to rein the surgeon in, restrain him, lest, in his enthusiasm, the surgeon endanger life. These surrogates are the conscience of the operating room. They, the statesmen. We, the warriors.

¡Milagro! It is Iris who is the patient on the operating table. A last-minute cancellation. An infant with too low a blood count, crackles in his lungs. An anesthesiologist has said no. The infant's misfortune is Iris's good luck. Now we are in the middle of the surgery. The skin flaps have been cut. A full-thickness skin graft has been taken from the girl's groin. There is still much to do.

Anesthetist: "How much longer will you be at it?"
Surgeon: "Another hour and a half or so. Why?"
Anesthetist: "The trouble is . . . we are almost out of oxygen. The tank is on EMPTY."
Surgeon: "No."
Anesthetist: "Yes."
Surgeon (angrily): "How could you let that happen?" Then,
"We'll have to find a good place to stop."
Anesthetist: "That would be *right now*. I'm going to have to wake her up."
Surgeon: "Can you wait one minute?"
Anesthetist: "No."

Just then, the door to the operating room opens and a huge headless tank is rolled, wobbled, carried even, into the room. Two tiny Peruvian nurses are supplying the brawn. They are dwarfed by the giant tank. Still, they use their breasts and their breath to propel it forward. A monkey wrench is found and the tubing is switched from the dead tank to this new one. A knob is turned. All eyes are on the gauge. No one knows how much, if any, oxygen the tank holds. The needle pops to the halfway mark. It is enough. The surgeon and the anesthetist breathe heavily as though it were they who had run out of air.

Surgeon: "Now can we get on with it?"
Anesthetist: "Trouble is, now there's no oxygen in the recovery room. This is their tank. The only one."
Surgeon: "Suture!"

I am invited to the operating room of a Peruvian surgeon to observe and comment. The room and everything in it sparkle. The walls, ceiling, linen—all white. The surgeon is a flamboyant older man with a gray moustache. He speaks no English but explains each step of the procedure at a shout; I might be deaf. I shout back at him in rudimentary Spanish.

"*¡Bisturí!*" he calls out to the scrub nurse at his elbow. And, making a quick small Sign of the Cross over the woman's belly with the scalpel, he makes a huge deep incision in the upper-right abdomen. None of the bleeders is clamped. Unaccountably, they stop after a minute or so. The Sign of the Cross?

"*Gorda,*" growls the surgeon. Her fat annoys him. He looks up at me and shakes his head, asking commiseration from a colleague. I shake my head in return.

"*Muchissima gorda,*" I say and cluck my tongue hard. His two assistants speak only when spoken to. Nor do they perform any single step of the operation but stand holding what he tells them to hold with an obedience that is as remarkable as it is absolute. I think of the backtalk I get in New Haven, where I am lucky to be let into the operating room at all, and then must painstakingly attend to each intern and resident according to his level of experience. They would settle for nothing less. Nor would I, actually. It is the American way. Youth is stroked and cosseted. But here in Peru it is age, petulant, cantankerous age, that commands. I rather like the idea.

"*¡Cálculo in choledochus!*" the surgeon shouts at me.

"*¡Sí! Sí!*" I shout back. He opens the common bile duct, scoops out several spoonsful of sludge and gravel, then tries to pass a dilator down through it into the duodenum. It will not go.

"*¿Otro cálculo?*" I suggest.

"*¡No!*" he thunders. "*¡Espasmo!*" It is the anesthetist's fault somehow. The surgeon informs the hapless anesthetist that in America he is quite certain that the anesthetist is helpful to the surgeon, that he does not become part of the problem. Abashed, the anesthetist checks the patient's blood pressure and injects something into the intravenous tubing. More passes with the dilator. At last it goes through the narrows into the intestine.

"*Muchas gracias,*" I tell him. "A beautiful job."

"I do another one tomorrow," he hollers in Spanish. "You must come and watch me."

In the central corridor of the operating suite, next to a wall, stands a small gaudy altar, no more than a crucifix on a tablecloth strewn with artificial flowers. No one pays it the slightest attention. But it is there. In the same tiny storeroom that is stuffed with the cartons of our equipment, the men and women of INTERPLAST dress and undress together. We have not the modesty of the Peruvians who seem shocked by our shamelessness. Here too, between operations, we chew away at the slabs of tough fried meat and buns that are handed out by a beautiful young woman who is always dressed to the nines for the occasion—flowered silk dress and high heels. What could she possibly be thinking? Someone takes the roll of toilet paper from the table and disappears. Already, for our sins, the diarrhea rages.

¡Emergencia! One of the palates done yesterday is bleeding. A nurse wheels the rattletrap gurney through the doors of the *sala de operaciones*. The boy, Juan, is eleven years old. A gauze has been stuffed into his mouth. The end protrudes and is draped over his chin. It is blood-soaked and more blood drips from it to his bare chest. With one finger, as he has been instructed, he presses the wad against the roof of his mouth. He is utterly calm in his martyrdom. We place him on his side on the operating table. He will be put to sleep in that position, tilted forward, in order to prevent blood from running into his windpipe. A mask is held over his face. Above it, dark slanted eyes gaze at something far beyond the swirl of doctors, nurses and equipment in which he is engulfed. Only once does he raise one hand to point to the angle of his jaw where the anesthetist is pressing too tightly.

"Your finger is hurting him," someone says.

"Sorry," the anesthetist says to the boy. "How do you say 'I'm sorry' in Spanish?"

"Never mind. He speaks only Quechua, anyway. He's from a village far up. Not even Pizzaro got to it." Only when the boy is asleep and the tube is secure in his airway is he turned on his back. The packing is removed from his mouth. It is chased by a red froth, then pure blood.

"I see it," says the anesthetist. We peer into the open mouth of the boy and we too see the torn artery at the front of the incision in his palate. Two four-by-four-inch gauze pads have been unfolded and packed in the throat to prevent aspiration. A metal mouth gag is inserted behind the front teeth and screwed open. Now the site of hemorrhage can be seen with ease. Tick, tick, ticking away. With each beat of the pulse another expensive red jet. A single stitch of 4-0 vicryl in a figure-of-eight, and we are dry. We are safe. The anesthetist holds out his hand which is completely painted with blood.

"Can someone wash me off?"

A nurse or a doctor, like an artist, must have an illiberal human heart, the kind that is unmoved by news of a far-off massacre, in Cambodia, say, but breaks each time at the death of Juliet. Juan is wheeled to the recovery room, his mouth still stuffed with gauze packing. The lump is in *my* throat.

I am scheduled to remove an Indian woman's gallbladder at 8:00 A.M. All night my own abdominal griping has spiraled to truly marvelous heights, my bowels vibrating like a harp. An operation performed under such intestinal duress is likely to become a photo-finish race. How I envy the antibodies of the roomful of Peruvian doctors and students who have gathered to assist and observe. And how I curse my insipid Connecticut colon. In the room where I work no one speaks English. We shall see. The patient is a short chunk of a woman somewhere between thirty and fifty years of age.

"*¿Donde le duele?*" I ask her. "Where does it hurt?" She points to her gallbladder. I press the area firmly. She winces. "O.K.," I say eloquently.

The anesthetic is peridural; she is to be awake. Still, she has descended into a mysterious condition of apartness from the world. She is elsewhere. My assistants and I scrub in silence. Masked, gowned, gloved, we are no longer able to use the sign language that has sufficed for conversation heretofore. The abdomen has been prepared.

"*¡Bisturí!*" I say, holding my hand for the scalpel. There is a sudden quick slice. But it takes place somewhere within my own belly. The diarrhea. A wave of faintness is fought down. There is to be none of that, I tell myself. And we start. Dense adhesions obliterate the gallbladder as completely as the fog on that first day hid the airport of Arequipa. There is more bleeding than I like.

"Jesus," I say in English. "She is bleeding all over South America." I say it again, this time, for some reason, in French. Then it is that María, the scrub nurse, who has up to now been silent, says, all but inaudibly, "*Je parle français.*"

Her very words are hemostatic for the patient, antidiarrhetic for me. From then on I speak to her in French which she translates into Spanish for the others.

"*Il y a beaucoup de calculs, calculs grands et petits, dans le cholécyste, mais rien dans le choledochus.*" I listen to her repeating these things in Spanish.

"*Je préfère deux ligatures de coton pour le canal cystique.*" Again, she interprets.

"*Les jeunes filles de Peru sont très charmantes,*" I drone on. María gives a tiny giggle and says nothing.

"*Mais, traduisez, s'il vous plaît.*" With obvious reluctance, she does. The men in the room laugh appreciatively.

"*Et María est mon ange gardien. Traduisez.*" This last with all the sadism of a conquistador. With a sweet blend of pleasure and pain, she does. The surgeon rules here, remember? More laughter, after which María and the men have at each other in high spirits. I see that she is more than a match for the whole lot. Whatever nerves I had before are now settled. The gallbladder is quickly and

231

neatly removed. Without untoward event, as we say in surgery.

"*Felicitaciones. Muchas gracias. Perfecto.*"

I peel off my gown and gloves and race to the toilet.

The Indians chew coca leaves wrapped about a small piece of limestone. The wad is held in the groove between the cheek and the gum. It is the slow activation of the cocaine by the stone and saliva that serves to disconnect, just a bit, the chewer from his hardships. Such usage does not make him happy, nor is it meant to. Only to alleviate. Very sensible, we decide. At the hospital, in the long waiting lines, the eyes of the coca eaters are withdrawn, unfocused. It does seem true that in every culture there is some national elixir to which the people turn for their dreams and for relief. In the spirit of experimentation, shall we say, we pay a little money to a man outside Turistas. Within minutes there are pebbles, there are leaves. In the evening, self-consciously, we try to feel what it is that they feel. *Nada.* Only, we cannot sleep. And so we go to Pena, the native cabaret. Bottles of pisco on the tables. The nurses and doctors with whom, hours earlier, we had shared disappointment and triumph in the operating rooms teach us to dance. Germán Muñoz, a specialist in the treatment of burns, Luis and Alfredo who dream of going abroad to finish their surgical training; Luis, to the States; Alfredo, to Brazil. And the nurses, María, Eleana and the rest, clapping their hands to the beat, now and then uttering tiny birdlike cries, their eyes gone muzzy with longing. We watch them court each other, the men all gallantry, the women a blend of eagerness and coquetry. Here at Pena, it is INTERPLAST that is shy, awkward, encased in a Puritan cuirass that holds stiff our hips and shoulders and necks. We marvel at the oiled hinges of our counterparts. At last midnight, and with it, lubrication. Then we too come ashake and aswivel. The music is made with wooden flutes, reed pipes, guitars and drums. It is immensely erotic, feral. The flutes and pipes cry, shriek, moan. The guitars shuffle chords this way and that. But it is the great drum that governs. Like a cardiac muscle it drives our blood. When, abruptly, the beat changes, we suffer arrhythmia.

Don is assisting a local surgeon, Alfredo Montes, in the repair of a cleft lip. Alfredo is the single most important man here for it is he, if anyone, who will inherit the mantle. In a few days INTERPLAST will have departed. Alfredo will be left to carry on. He is immensely Peruvian—short, beefy, brown, with a wealth of black hair which he has had "styled." There are gold chains around his neck.

"Tinte," says Alfredo to the scrub nurse, and with a sharp stylet dipped in ink he marks out the flaps on the mound of chaotic flesh.

"No, no," says Don. "Make it longer laterally. Look. Here is the vermilion border. That's the Cupid's bow. Yeah, now you've got it. Bravissimo!" An hour later, Alfredo is suturing the two halves of the orbicularis oris muscle, the one used in pouting, sucking, sipping, kissing, all of that. With each suture he restores a new function to that mouth. Minutes later, the flattened nostril rises in a lovely curve to match that of the other side. The defect narrows, is closed. Over the head of the child, the American and Peruvian shake gloved hands. This, then, from Don: "Give a man a fish and he will eat one meal. Teach him how to fish and he will not be hungry the rest of his life. And he will feed others." He is given to adages.

"Old sawbones," I say.

Next to the hospital is a kind of Indian funeral parlor. It is a canny choice of location. We are walking past when a man emerges carrying a flat limp bundle wrapped in a blue alpaca blanket. He is followed by a woman with a more than usually solemn face. She has the inevitable protruding abdomen and wide pelvis of the Indian female. These women are masterpieces of fecundity. Many go decades without menstruating once, proceeding directly from lactation to pregnancy. Aida says it is one way of saving on sanitary napkins. The woman is wearing a stiff short skirt of many colors. It has the shape of an elongated tutu. But the shape only. Beneath, wide-set skinny rachitic legs. An ancient battered car is waiting. The man tries to insert the bundle into the backseat, but cannot. The bundle is too long. After a few clumsy attempts, he gives it up, opens the trunk of the car and lays the bundle inside. Just before he closes the lid, we see five small dark toes emerging from the blanket. The sound of the trunk closing is the most utterly serious sound in the world. The man and woman get into the car and are driven away. We stare at the trunk of the car until it is out of sight. A few steps from where the car had stood, the topiary garden of Honorio Delgado Hospital needs clipping badly. The once crisp green creatures have quite gone to seed. The little llama is whiskered; the angel, shaggy. My own melancholy is a foot thick.

I am walking in the city with Don.
"Clean, isn't it?" he says. "No discarded paper or plastic in the streets. No dog shit." And it is true. Not Paris, but Arequipa is the city of light. If blue skies, herds of mountains, sprays of stars and clean streets are proof of divine approval, then God surely loves Arequipa. Praise how you will the city that boasts the Cathedral of Notre Dame; if to walk there with unsoiled shoes you have to keep your eyes on the pavement and practice a kind of broken-field running, it just isn't worth it. In Arequipa the dogs are

confined to rooftops and courtyards. In Arequipa in the evening, you can walk and look up at the stars.

Sunday, Carlos Galda, the chief of surgery, has arranged an outing for us at a restored Inca grain mill. After weeks of surgery, clinics and rounds, we are eager for leisure. We are a caravan of four cars each holding five *interplásticos*. There is much hilarity. At *El Molino* there will be a feast; octopus marinated in lime juice, slices of charcoal-broiled beef heart, pisco and beer. And dancing without which a party is not a party in Peru. Peruvians cannot imagine a party where people sit around and converse. What fun is that? they ask. Not much, we admit. The mill is about twenty miles from Arequipa, in the country. I am in the backseat of the last car. Near the halfway mark we cross a narrow bridge that spans a deep gorge at the bottom of which is a swiftly running river. Immediately having crossed, we find that the road ascends sharply, then curves out of sight. The leading cars have already disappeared from view. It is in mid-ascent of that incline that Fate casts upon INTERPLAST its most ironic smile. The car stalls. Before the hand brake can be applied, we have rolled backward a few feet and struck a small car filled with people. It is an ancient blue Volkswagen. The driver of that Volkswagen leaps from the car, neglecting, in his ardor for battle, to close the door. Now he and our driver are fully engaged in a passionate discussion which promises to be interminable. I get out of the car to assess the damages. None to our car, I see; a dent, only, in the front bumper of the other. Never mind, I say. I'll give him money. Let's get going. Just then, thinking to disengage us from the Volkswagen, our driver releases the hand brake prior to starting the motor. It is a lapse. The hand brake is reapplied but not before we have once again nudged the Volkswagen. This time, it begins to roll backward down the hill toward the bridge. I chase after it, thinking, I suppose, to reach in and pull up the hand brake. But I cannot catch the car. Faster and faster it rolls. Through the windshield I see the faces of the passengers. Indians. Their eyes are wide with terror. Their mouths are open for shrieking. Just before the bridge, the little blue car takes a small sickening turn to the left, achieves the rim of the chasm, tips up at the front and plunges backward into the ravine. All this I watch from a few feet away. And hear the crash far below. For a moment I pause at the edge, then leap. The sides of the gorge are not quite straight. There are stunted shrubs to grab, rocks to brace a foot against. It is an utterly graceless scramble downward, at least half of which is made on skidding buttocks, heels. A series of bounces, really, until that final plummet into the river. A mouthful of raw sewage.

I am twenty feet from the rock ledge where the car has come to rest on its side. From the wreck, whimpering. They are alive! I see three old men. They are covered with blood. The river beneath the ledge is red with it. I try to pull one of the men through a window, but he is wedged. Now I am joined by Bill and Michael. They are both young and strong. I am merely old and reckless. We shout to each other above the noise of the river. Our voices echo against the walls of the chasm. The air is stagnant, palpable. Michael climbs on top of the car and tries to open the door. It will not open. He pounds it with his fist, a rock. At last it gives, and we hand the three old men out to each other. They are Franciscan monks. They wear long brown habits and rosaries. Somehow, this makes it worse. From the bridge, people throw ponchos in which the injured will be carried up to the road. Other men have come down to help. One of the monks has sustained an avulsion of his forehead and scalp. Blood from the great wound films his face. He is blinded by it. I wipe the wound with my hand, find the artery that is spurting at the base of the gouge, pinch it between thumbnail and fingernail. The bleeding slows, virtually stops. We lay him on a poncho and begin to climb. He is immensely heavy and I must use one hand to pinch the artery. The other is the tiredest hand of my life. No mountaineer ever looked more longingly at the summit of Everest than I at the bridge high above. Crampons! I cry, like a surgeon calling for his favorite scalpel. What I want more than anything in the world is to lie down too, and, lapped in alpaca, be carried up the cliff. But there is that damned artery. And I its hemostat. Is it not, I ask myself . . . is it not the calling of a surgeon to be an instrument that the patient takes up in order to heal himself?

There are no level places, no footholds. Only slanting slippery rocks. Nor can we see the placement of our feet. Has human foot ever stepped here? I wonder. Will it ever again?

"Let's stop for a minute," says Bill. "Set him down." I could weep with relief. Twice we stop to rest, panting. Each time, we turn to look down. Beneath our feet the terrific cliff sinks in awful steepness to the river fifty . . . a hundred feet below. Who cares if it is fifty? Or a hundred? Or five hundred? The insolence of mere numbers. At last we reach the top; I unpinch my fingers from the blood vessel. The bleeding has stopped. It does not resume. The three wounded men are placed in the back of a truck and taken to Honorio Delgado. The next day we will visit them on rounds. Rows of cotton sutures will crisscross their smiles. From swollen purple mouths they will cast blessings upon us. There will be no single word of reproach. All the same we will be filled with guilt. We who came to repair and have ended by damaging. Conquistadores!

But now, still standing at a cowardly distance from the edge of the ravine, I piece together the fragments of my body, which is not that of your fit and fly-soled athlete come to Peru to scale the *cordillera blanca* but that of a middle-aged padder of pavement. No, I am not one of those macho surgeons who give themselves airs over muscular prowess. Great aprons of beef do not hang from my diminutive skeleton. Ah well, Carlos and the others have come back to find us. He insists that we go on to El Molino. Shattered, and so malleable, we do. You do not refuse a Peruvian's hospitality, no matter what.

The stairways and corridors of El Molino have been decorated with paper lanterns. Just outside, a herd of alpaca graze by a peaceful stream. There is kindly massage, tumblers of pisco. And dancing. In two hours we are tipsy. Later, on the way back to Arequipa, we stop at the bridge and go to stand again at the edge of the precipice. A rank air hisses up from the depths. Like ones who have emerged from the mouth of Hell, we are returned to a state of childhood horror. You are making too much of it, we say to one another. And know that we are making far too little. We pick up stones and toss them over the side. The one I throw takes hours to strike the bottom. It has a muffled sound like the impact of flesh. A noise like that could kill you. I would not go down there again for Saint Francis himself.

A last visit to Honorio Delgado. What a far cry it is from my sleek and spanking hospital in New Haven—all glass and prestressed concrete. And yet, so like. A hospital is only a building until you hear the slate hooves of dreams galloping upon its roof. You listen then and know that here is no mere pile of stone and precisely cut timber but an inner space full of pain and relief. Such a place invites mankind to heroism. For us, Honorio Delgado has become an instrument with which to confront life, a rock that stands firm against the incessant lapping of fate. Even at Pena, at the mill, at the bottom of the ravine, this hospital clung to us like a she-wolf. We could smell her maternal odors penetrating to our hearts. Tomorrow we leave Peru carrying with us the pathetic belief that the way to heal the world is to take it in for repairs. One on one. One at a time.